the
little
book
of
Australia

the little book of Australia

DAVID DALE

ALLEN&UNWIN

Allen & Unwin
83 Alexander Street
Crows Nest NSW 2065
Australia

Phone:	(61 2) 8425 0100
Fax:	(61 2) 9906 2218
Email:	info@allenandunwin.com
Web:	www.allenandunwin.com

Cataloguing-in-Publication details are available
from the National Library of Australia
www.librariesaustralia.nla.gov.au

ISBN 978 1 237 211 2

Internal design by Design By Committee
Typeset by Midland Typesetters, Australia
Printed in Australia by McPherson's Printing Group

10 9 8 7 6 5 4 3 2 1

Contents

Introduction

In offering this little tract to the public it is equally the writer's wish to conduce to their amusement and information. That was the opening sentence of the first book ever published about Australia.* The same motivations are behind *this* little tract 220 years later. But as well as wanting to amuse and inform, I'd add a third ambition: to provoke. I hope this book will get readers thinking and talking about Australia's identity.

I started this project because I kept hearing politicians and pundits going on about what 'the average Australian' wants, believes, expects, fears and won't stand for. In the mid-Noughties, they suddenly discovered the importance of teaching 'Australian values' to recent arrivals, and they started labelling certain actions, opinions or people as 'un-Australian'.

It seemed to me that most of their generalisations were based on guesswork, prejudice or wishful thinking, and hardly ever on facts. I thought it might be useful to do a reality check, to bring together all the information a person might need in order to speculate about national values and to ask whether there is—or ever could be—an average, normal or typical way of living here. Those politicians and pundits seemed keen to enforce standardisation. I was keen to describe diversity. I was particularly curious about how, in just 50 years, this country transformed itself from one of the dullest places on the planet to one of the most interesting.

There were plenty of history books about Australia, and plenty of books about scenery, but very few books about what kind of people 21st-century Australians might be. You can tell a lot about a nation from the ways it shops, competes, talks, eats,

* Watkin Tench's A *Narrative of the Expedition to Botany Bay*, (discussed on page 152).

laughs, worships and entertains itself. So I set about charting our favourite movies, world records, political passions, changing language, popular products, and the characters we celebrate or satirise.

My research led to the publication in 2006 of *Who We Are: A miscellany of the new Australia*, updated in 2007 as *Who We Are: A snapshot of Australia today*. Then came an election, the apology to Aboriginal people, a baby boom, the iPhone, a global financial crisis, Utegate and a national obsession with *MasterChef*. Clearly the book needed more than an update. So what you're holding is rewritten, reconsidered, reconstructed, retitled and 50 pages longer than the prototype.

There's a bit of history here but it's mainly about how we're doing one-tenth of the way through the 21st century—a reality that may be somewhat different from the myths Australians hold about their land. You'll find mention of lamingtons, Holden cars, Don Bradman, beer, funnel-webs, Nellie Melba and *The Man from Snowy River*. But you'll also find pad Thai, *Underbelly*, sauvignon blanc, Bob Brown, climate change, Schappelle Corby and *The Dark Knight*—which may be more relevant to the national identity in 2010.

One of our healthiest traits is a habit of making fun of ourselves. Australians are uncomfortable with displays of patriotism. They'd rather trim tall poppies than trumpet their triumphs. So when I say there are a few things in this book that made me feel surprised and proud, please don't spread it around.

We know we're good at sport and good at acting, but I don't think we've ever seen ourselves as a land of visionary idealists. Yet you can't help getting that impression when you read the inspiring speeches in Chapter 4 and the sections on Stirrers, Investigators, Helpers and Pioneers in Chapter 6. And if you look at Inventions in Chapter 2, you suspect there may be a national aptitude for inventing creative solutions to practical problems.

But any heart swellings this book may stir are incidental to its primary purpose, which is to be a practical reference guide and a settler of bets for every household, office, pub, council chamber and newsroom, so that future debates about who we are don't have to be conducted in ignorance. The best advice I can give you at this point is: **USE THE INDEX**. It's at least as good as google.

Many people and institutions helped my research. The regular reports of the Australian Bureau of Statistics were my primary source, particularly 'Social Trends' and 'Measures of Social Progress', but I also learned much from ACNielsen, the Motion Picture Distributors Association of Australia, OzTAM, Roy Morgan Research, the Australian Record Industry Association, GTK Australia and the Audit Bureau of Circulations. My reference works included *The Macquarie Encyclopedia of Australian Events* (Macquarie Library), *2006 Fact Finder* (Hardie Grant), *Well May We Say … The Speeches That Made Australia* (Black Inc), *Advance Australia … Where?*, by Hugh Mackay (Hachette), *The Dinkum Dictionary* by Susan Butler (Text Publishing) and *Stirring Australian Speeches* (Melbourne University Press).

I also need to thank the readers of my columns, 'Who We Are' in *The Sun Herald*, and 'The Tribal Mind' in *The Sydney Morning Herald*. Their thoughtful responses to my blog (http://blogs.sunherald.com.au/whoweare) spurred me on to new inquiries and corrected many a misapprehension.

At Allen & Unwin, I'm grateful to Patrick Gallagher for funding the initial project and for reincarnating it in bigger and better form, Alex Nahlous for editing and Josh Durham for the design. My banderilleros Susan Anthony, Hugh MacKay, Ian Garland, Katherine Thomson, Tony Dorigo and Lucio Galletto raised issues I needed to explain. And my wife Susan and daughter Millie offered patience and encouragement beyond the call of duty.

But any errors or oversights are all my own work, and I'd love to correct them. If you feel there are other insights into this country that really ought to be discussed here, send them to me at bookofaustralia@gmail.com and I'll do the research. Between us we can turn the next edition of *LBA* into this country's definitive source of amusement, information and provocation.

David Dale
January, 2010

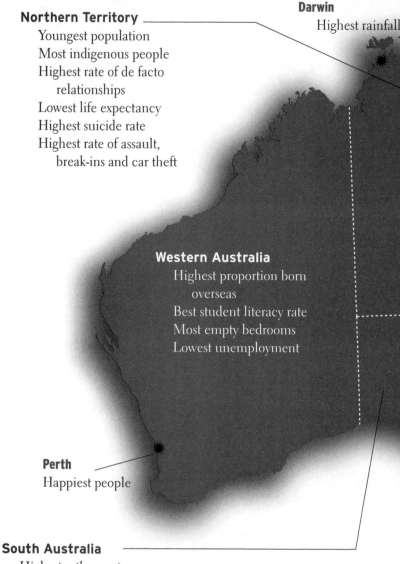

Northern Territory
Youngest population
Most indigenous people
Highest rate of de facto
relationships
Lowest life expectancy
Highest suicide rate
Highest rate of assault,
break-ins and car theft

Darwin
Highest rainfall

Western Australia
Highest proportion born
overseas
Best student literacy rate
Most empty bedrooms
Lowest unemployment

Perth
Happiest people

South Australia
Highest asthma rate
Highest home ownership rate
Most lone-person households
Lowest marriage rate
Highest sport attendance
Oldest population

Victoria
Lowest birth rate
Highest drug-induced
death rate
Highest car
ownership rate

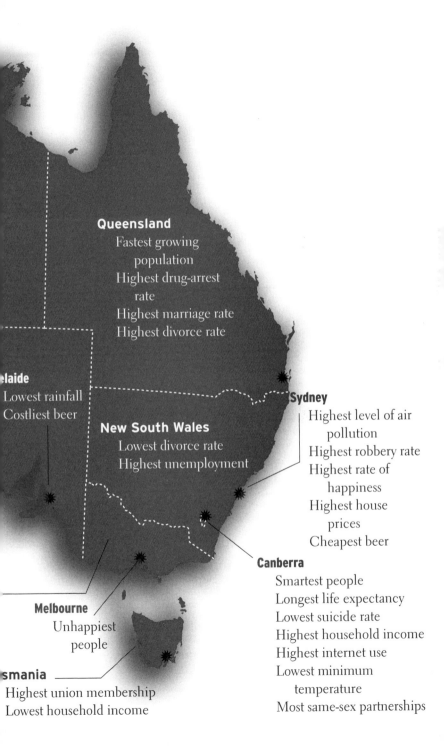

Queensland
Fastest growing
population
Highest drug-arrest
rate
Highest marriage rate
Highest divorce rate

elaide
Lowest rainfall
Costliest beer

New South Wales
Lowest divorce rate
Highest unemployment

Sydney
Highest level of air
pollution
Highest robbery rate
Highest rate of
happiness
Highest house
prices
Cheapest beer

Canberra
Smartest people
Longest life expectancy
Lowest suicide rate
Highest household income
Highest internet use
Lowest minimum
temperature
Most same-sex partnerships

Melbourne
Unhappiest
people

smania
Highest union membership
Lowest household income

THE BITS THAT MAKE US

FIRST GLANCE

Born in Australia: 78 per cent of the population
Aboriginal: 2.3 per cent
Born in Britain: 6 per cent
Born in New Zealand: 4 per cent
Born in China or Vietnam: 4 per cent
Born in Italy or Greece: 3 per cent
Born in the Middle East: 0.7 per cent
Speaking a language other than English at home: 15 per cent

Catholic: 26 per cent
Anglican: 19 per cent
Other Christian: 19 per cent
Buddhist: 2.1 per cent
Muslim: 1.7 per cent
Hindu: 0.5 per cent
Jewish: 0.4 per cent
No religion: 19 per cent
Unspecified: 11 per cent

Aged over 37: 50 per cent
In a partnership, with children under 16: 38 per cent
Living alone: 9 per cent

Living within 50 kilometres of the sea: 85 per cent
Living on a farm: 1 per cent
Owning or paying off a home: 70 per cent
Living in a home with three or more bedrooms: 75 per cent
Proportion of three-bedroom homes containing one or two people: 58 per cent
Homeless: 0.5 per cent
Likely to cohabit before marriage: 74 per cent of couples
Likely to get divorced: 43 per cent of marriages

Having a beyond-school qualification (degree, diploma etc): 51 per cent of adults
Income of less than $600 a week after tax: 50 per cent of adults
Donating to charity at least once a year: 77 per cent of adults (average $424 per Australian household)
Doing volunteer work to help others: 33 per cent

Smokers: 20 per cent of adults (but 33 per cent of men aged 25 to 34)
Use marijuana: 11 per cent
Use ecstasy: 3 per cent
Drink alcohol at health-risk level: 13 per cent

Classified as obese: 25 per cent of adults
Classified as overweight: 37 per cent of adults
Feeling in good or excellent health: 85 per cent
Exercise for fitness: 65 per cent
With a disability requiring help at home: 11 per cent
Experienced a mental disorder (depression, anxiety, phobia, drug abuse) in the past year: 20 per cent

Feel safe at home alone after dark: 86 per cent
Feel safe walking alone after dark: 46 per cent

Likely to be the victim of a personal crime this year: 11 per cent
Moved house in the past five years: 43 per cent
Have access to a car: 86 per cent

Own a mobile phone: 92 per cent of people over 14
Go to the cinema more than twice a year: 67 per cent

Have a microwave: 90 per cent of homes
Have a DVD player: 85 per cent of homes
Have at least one computer: 75 per cent of homes (of whom 60 per cent have broadband internet access)
Have two or more TV sets: 70 per cent of homes
Have a dishwasher: 42 per cent of homes
Subscribe to pay TV: 30 per cent of homes

THIS YEAR

302 000 people will be born in Australia.

501 000 will arrive, intending to stay for more than a year.

224 000 will leave, intending to stay away for more than a year.

143 000 will die: 29 per cent from cancer, 20 per cent from heart disease, and 9 per cent from stroke.

236 000 will get married.

96 000 will get divorced.

392 000 will move from one state to another.

685 000 women will be single parents with dependent children.

139 500 men will be single parents with dependent children.

3.3 million will be at school.

1.4 million will work in the retail trade.

1.1 million will work in manufacturing.

370 000 will work in agriculture.

6.5 million will buy and sell shares.

23 820 will be in prison: 22 180 men and 1640 women.

90 000 abortions will be performed in hospitals and private clinics.

800 000 new cars will be bought: 21 per cent Toyota, 19 per cent Holden, 14 per cent Ford, 7 per cent Nissan, 6 per cent Mitsubishi.

13.4 million vehicles will be registered.

14 600 kilometres, the equivalent of two return trips from Sydney to Perth, will be covered by the average car.

1560 people will be killed by cars.

5.2 million travellers from overseas, mainly from New Zealand, Britain, Japan, the US, Korea, China and Singapore, will enter the country, staying, on average, 27 nights.

3.5 million trips overseas will be made by Australians, mainly to New Zealand, Britain, the US, China and Fiji.

12.5 million credit cards will be used to spend $165 billion, with an average outstanding debt of $3100 per cardholder.

82 million cinema tickets will be sold.

94 million hens and roosters, 93 million sheep, 29 million cattle and 2.7 million pigs will share the continent with us.

1.3 million tonnes of potatoes (64 kg per person) will be consumed, along with 449 000 tonnes of tomatoes, 272 000 tonnes of carrots, 496 000 tonnes of oranges, 276 500 tonnes of apples and 177 000 tonnes of bananas.

HOW MANY OF US

As of 26 January 2010, **the population of Australia** was 22 140 000. According to the Australian Bureau of Statistics, this figure rises by one person every 1 minute and 12 seconds (or 1200 a day). On average, there is a birth every 1 minute and 44 seconds, a death every 3 minutes and 39 seconds, and a net gain of one international immigrant every 1 minute and 53 seconds.

Our population grows at 1.7 per cent a year (faster than Indonesia's, at 1.2 per cent, and India's, at 1.6 per cent). But some parts of the country are more popular than others: this decade the populations of Western Australia and Queensland have been growing at 2.5 per cent a year. **The fastest-growing areas** in the land are Perth, Cairns, Brisbane, the Gold Coast and Moreton Bay (just north of Brisbane).

The bureau predicts that Australia will reach 30 million by 2025 and 38 million by 2050. Entrepreneurs think we should aim to reach 50 million, the tipping point to make us a world economic player. Environmentalists think we should reduce our population because the continent's resources can't sustain more than 18 million people. The bureau says neither of those scenarios can be achieved this century.

If your idea of fun is to watch big numbers changing, go to www.abs.gov.au and click on 'Australia's population'. There you'll find the Bureau's nifty people clock. It will send you to other sites which reveal that Australia is the 55th most populated country in the world (**China** is top with 1.35 billion) and the 12th most spacious country in the world (**Russia** is biggest with 17 million square kilometres, while we have 7.7 million). We have one of the lowest population densities: 2.8 people per square kilometre, compared with Singapore with 6390 per square kilometre.

MATING HABITS

This sounds like good news: 95 per cent of Australians find **love** at some point in their lives, and 25 per cent find love twice. Those excellent odds were calculated by the Bureau of Statistics, which noted in 2009 that 61 per cent of adult Australians were currently living with a partner, and half of those relationships had lasted 18 years or more. It continued:

'According to the Family Characteristics and Transitions Survey, 84 per cent of adults had had at least one marriage or de facto relationship. For people aged 35 years or over, 95 per cent had had at least one marriage or de facto relationship. This included 18 per cent who had had two (live-in) relationships and 7 per cent who had three or more.'

These are some other conclusions we feel safe in drawing from the Bureau's research:

Australians like to try before they buy. The bureau puts it more politely: 'Almost three quarters (74 per cent) of people who married in the 2000s lived together before marrying.' And pregnancy no longer summons the shotgun. 'In the five years to 2007, close to one third (32 per cent) of all births have been to unmarried mothers, twice the average rate of the 1980s.'

Once bitten, twice shy. The romantic boffins at the bureau have found that: 'People in de facto relationships who had been married before were significantly less likely to marry their new partner than people who had never been married. Around one quarter (26 per cent) of people in a de facto relationship who were separated, divorced or widowed intended to marry their current partner, compared with 50 per cent of people who had never been married.'

Men trade in older partners for younger models. In the average heterosexual partnership, the man is 2.6 years older than the woman. But, says the bureau, 'for marriages occurring between a male divorcee and a never married bride, the groom was, on average, older by 7.3 years'. Divorced women seeking toy boys have not been so lucky: 'Where the bride was remarrying after a divorce, she was around a year older than her never married groom.'

If you're looking for love, get more education. Australians mostly bond with people who have the same educational background. The bureau warns: 'Men with a lower level of education were more likely to have never partnered (10.4 per cent of men with no tertiary qualifications compared with 5 per cent of those with tertiary qualifications). Men who were not working in 2006–2007 were almost three times as likely to have never had a live-in relationship as those who were employed.'

If you can't find an atheist or a Buddhist, a Christian will do. Australians bond with people who share their religion — or lack of it. The bureau says 87 per cent of couplings are between people of the same belief system. These are the exceptions: 'Only 34 per cent of couples involving a Buddhist were same-faith partnerships. A higher proportion were "Buddhist-Christian" couples (40 per cent). Of the 26 per cent of couples involving at least one person with no religion, 52 per cent were matches where both partners were non-religious, while most of the remainder (46 per cent) were a "no religion-Christian" couple.'

Most marriages end in death. That's another way of saying that around 40 per cent end in divorce. The divorce rate has been declining over this decade, which looks like good news until you realise it's because the marriage rate was declining over the previous decade.

The seven-year itch is a myth. It's actually the 8 years and 11 months itch. For marriages that have ended in Australia, that's been the average gap between joining and separating.

Men are more annoying than women. That's what we can conclude from the fact that wives are far more likely to end relationships than are husbands. In 2008, 12 979 divorces were initiated by men, 16 613 were joint projects and 17 617 were initiated by women.

A terminated de facto relationship is likely to last two years, while a terminated marriage is likely to last nine years. The bureau looks on the bright side: 'In considering the apparently brief duration of de facto relationships, it should be kept in mind that this median is only for those relationships that have ended—a greater number have gone on to become a registered marriage or remain as long-term partnerships. In addition, where de facto relationships are being used by couples as a step before marriage, those that end before marriage may reduce the number of marriages that would otherwise end in divorce within a short period.' Which brings us back to try before you buy.

HOW ARE WE?

We're not hypochondriacs. A health survey of 22 000 Australians by the Bureau of Statistics in 2008 found 85 per cent saying they are in 'good', 'very good' or 'excellent' **health**. At the same time, 77 per cent claimed to have at least one long-term medical problem, and 40 per cent had three or more problems. The **most common disorders** described are:

1 **Long sightedness:** 26 per cent of the population
2 **Short sightedness:** 23 per cent
3 **Hay fever and allergic rhinitis:** 15 per cent
4 **Arthritis:** 15 per cent
5 **Back problems:** 14 per cent
6 **Long-term mental disorder:** 11 per cent
7 **Asthma:** 10 per cent
8 **Total/partial hearing loss:** 10 per cent
9 **High blood pressure:** 9 per cent
10 **High cholesterol:** 6 per cent
11 **Diabetes:** 4 per cent
12 **Osteoporosis:** 3 per cent

The major causes of death are:
1 **Cancer:** 29 per cent of deaths
2 **Heart disease:** 20 per cent
3 **Stroke:** 9 per cent
4 **Lung diseases:** 5 per cent
5 **Accidents:** 4 per cent
6 **Diabetes:** 2 per cent

The 2008 health survey also found these characteristics:

We love our little pills. While only 13 per cent of adults say they have 'high or very high psychological distress', 37 per cent say they used medication for 'mental wellbeing' in the past two weeks. Of these, 72 per cent were antidepressants and 27 per cent were sleeping tablets. Australia's favourite cheeruppers are vitamin supplements, followed by venlafaxine, citalopram and sertraline. We also relieve our mental worries in a liquid way: the proportion of people whose alcohol consumption is classified as high or risky has risen from 11 per cent in 2001 to 13 per cent in 2008.

We're kidding ourselves. When the bureau's researchers measured the people in the survey, they found that 68 per cent of men and 55 per cent of women could be classified as overweight or obese. But when people were asked to tell their measurements, only 63 per cent of men and 48 per cent of women gave answers that would suggest they were overweight or obese.

We treat our bodies shockingly. Some 54 per cent of men and 44 per cent of women eat one serving or less of fruit a day. As the bureau puts it, 95 per cent of men and 93 per cent of women have 'inadequate fruit or vegetable consumption' (less than the two-fruit, five-vegetable servings a day recommended by health authorities). In addition, 34 per cent of men and 36 per cent of women do no exercise of any kind.

We treat our kids as badly as we treat ourselves. Among children aged 5 to 17, 38 per cent eat less than one serving of fruit a day, and 37 per cent eat less than one serving of vegies a day; 17 per cent are overweight and 8 per cent are obese; 24 per cent of boys and 16 per cent of girls had consumed alcohol in the week before the interview, and of those, 6 per cent of boys and 7 per cent of girls were drinking at a risky or high level.

WHEN YOU'RE SMILING

Quick, on a scale from one to seven, rate how happy you are. Assume that 1 means 'I am delighted with my life' and 7 means 'I feel terrible'. Don't brood on it, just give an instant response. Ask the person nearest you to do the same.

If you rated your **happiness level** at 3 or better, you're with the vast mass of Australians — 82 per cent of us say we feel delighted, pleased or mostly satisfied with our lives. If your neighbour chose 5 or worse, she's in a tiny minority — only 3.5 per cent of Australians feel terrible, unhappy or mostly dissatisfied.

Yes, we're a cheery lot. In fact, we're cheerier in the late Noughties than we were in the late 90s. Back then, only 76 per cent of Australians rated their condition at 1, 2 or 3.

In 2007, the Bureau of Statistics interviewed a sample of 8800 Australians aged between 16 and 85 about their mental health. One question went like this: 'How do you feel about your life as a whole, taking into account what has happened in the last year and what you expect to happen in the future?' The sample was shown this list of possible responses: 1 Delighted; 2 Pleased; 3 Mostly satisfied; 4 Mixed; 5 Mostly dissatisfied; 6 Unhappy; 7 Terrible.

Out of the 16 million Australians in the age group studied, 2.8 million apparently float around in a state of delight and 5.4 million are smiling, while only 233 000 are unhappy and only 115 000 feel terrible. Here are the secrets of happiness . . .

Be old or young: The most miserable age group is people between 40 and 49. Of them, 3.7 per cent feel unhappy or terrible, compared with 1.5 per cent of people over 70 and

1.1 per cent of people aged 16 to 29. You might speculate that the 40-somethings have the dual worry of their dependent children turning into adults and their parents turning into dependent children.

Follow the sun. The bureau found that Brisbane and Perth were the happiest kingdoms of them all—55.7 per cent of people in each city rated themselves delighted or pleased. In Sydney, 50.8 per cent were delighted or pleased and 1.8 per cent felt unhappy or terrible. The most miserable city was Melbourne— only 47.9 per cent of south-easterners were delighted or pleased, while 3.1 per cent felt unhappy or terrible.

Pour another one. When happiness was compared with alcohol consumption, the drinkers won. Among people who had not consumed alcohol in the past 12 months, 44.7 per cent were delighted or pleased, and 3.8 per cent felt unhappy or terrible. Among people who described their alcohol consumption as 'At least once a week but less than nearly every day', the figures were 56.6 per cent happy and 1.4 per cent sad. But it's not a case of the more the merrier—among people who drink 'nearly every day', 47.2 per cent were happy and 3.2 per cent were sad.

Put out that fag. Among current smokers, 44.3 per cent were happy and 4.3 per cent were sad. Among non-smokers, 53.2 per cent were happy and 1.6 per cent were sad.

Get a degree. Among people who had gained an extra qualification after they left school, 54.8 per cent were happy, compared with 47 per cent of people who had only school qualifications.

Stay single or stay married. The happiness score was 53.7 per cent for married people and 53.2 per cent for never married people, but only 37.6 per cent for people who were separated, divorced or widowed.

Get on your feet. Among people who say they do a 'high level of exercise', 64.5 per cent are happy, while only 48.4 per cent of low exercisers are happy.

Get rich quick. Yes, money can buy happiness—57.3 per cent of people in the top 20 per cent of earnings say they are delighted or pleased, compared with 46.1 per cent of people in the bottom 20 per cent. But such is the level of optimism in this country that even the poor stay positive—only 3.7 per cent of the lowest earners say they feel unhappy or terrible. It's the lucky country, after all.

COMPARISONS: THEN AND NOW

Age
In 1901: 35 per cent of the population were under 15; 4 per cent were over 65; the median age was 22
Now: 20 per cent are under 15; 14 per cent are over 65, and the median age is 37

Life expectancy for males
In 1901: A baby boy could expect to live till 55 years of age
1935: life expectancy was 65
1980: 70
Now: 79

The mix
In 1901: 23 per cent of the population were born overseas (in Britain)
1947: 10 per cent were born overseas (in Britain)
Now: 22 per cent are overseas born (mainly in Britain, New Zealand, Italy, China, Vietnam, Greece, India and 180 other countries) and 25 per cent of people born here have at least one parent born overseas

Main source countries of immigrants (after Britain)
Arriving in 1962: Greece, Italy, Yugoslavia
1972: Lebanon, New Zealand, Yugoslavia
1982: Vietnam, New Zealand, South Africa
1992: New Zealand, China, Vietnam
Now: New Zealand, China, India

The stay-at-homes
In 1976: 21 per cent of 20- to 29-year-olds lived with their parents
Now: 30 per cent do

Marriage age
In 1976: The average age for men to marry was 25; for women 22
Now: It's 30 for men; 28 for women

The wedding service
In 1986: 61 per cent of marriages were performed in a church
Now: 40 per cent

Birth rate
In 1901: 4 babies were born per woman
1960: 3.5 per woman
1975: 2 per woman
Now: 1.8 babies are born per woman

In 1956: The median age for women giving birth was 23
1976: It was 26
Now: It's 30
In 1976: 40 per cent of 20- to 29-year-olds had children
Now: 16 per cent do

COMPARISONS: THEM AND US

Birth rate
Australia: 1.8 children per woman
Papua New Guinea: 4.1
Malaysia: 2.9
Indonesia: 2.4
America: 2.1
Britain: 1.7
Italy: 1.3

Murder rate
Australia: 1.9 per 100 000 people each year
South Africa: 55.9
America: 5.6
New Zealand: 2.5
Britain: 1.6
Italy: 1.5
Japan: 1.0

Median age of population
Australia: 37
Japan: 43
Italy: 42
Britain: 39
America: 36
Indonesia: 26
Papua New Guinea: 20

Life expectancy for females
Australia: A baby girl born now can expect to live till 84 years of age
Hong Kong: 85
Japan: 85
Italy: 83
Britain: 81
America: 80
Malaysia: 76
Indonesia: 69

COMPARISONS: MEN AND WOMEN

About 51 per cent of our population is female; 49 per cent is male. The difference happens because men die younger than women — in any year roughly 67 000 men will die compared with 62 000 women.

The life expectancy of a boy born this year is 79 and a girl is 84, unless they are Aboriginal, for whom the figures are 60 and 65 respectively.

The average weekly total earnings of women is $763; for men it's $1147. When hours and types of job are standardised, it appears that women, on average, earn 91 per cent of what men earn: an improvement from 78 per cent in the early 1970s.

Women hold 15 per cent of senior management jobs in Australian business. On average, a female full-time manager earns 25 per cent less than a male manager.

The Australian Bureau of Statistics tells us a woman is **more likely than a man to be:** old, living alone, at the movies, using a library, seeing a doctor, seeking a divorce, in a botanic garden, sexually assaulted, walking for exercise, doing more than 15 hours a week of unpaid housework, suffering arthritis and asthma, having a university degree, suffering a disability requiring help at home, and using contraception.

She is less likely than a man to be: murdered, beaten up, robbed, in gaol, watching a sporting event, deaf, playing golf, doing less than 5 hours a week of unpaid housework, dying of cancer or injured in an accident.

HOW CLEVER?

The term '**The Lucky Country**' was coined in the 1960s by the writer Donald Horne, and it wasn't a compliment. He meant that by a happy accident, Australians had stumbled onto resources that allowed us to prosper among world economies, and this meant we never noticed how badly we are managed. Here's his entire quote: 'Australia is a lucky country, run by second-rate people who share its luck.'

In the 1990s, Horne joined a campaign to raise education standards, aiming to make us a 'clever country' with the skills to thrive without props such as iron ore and coal. He said: 'I think we should realise that "the lucky country" provides a descriptive phrase, condemning Australia for what it was, whereas "the clever country" is a prescriptive phrase, suggesting to Australia what it might become.'

So are we there yet? The latest 'Social Trends' report from the Bureau of Stats has good news about the cleverness of young Australians. Here are the results of the latest testing on 8000 high school students in what is called TIMSS (Trends in International Mathematics and Science Study): 'Australian students performed well in 2007 when compared with other participating countries, but were outperformed by England, the United States and most of the Asian countries, especially Singapore and Chinese Taipei. Australian students achieved an international ranking of 14th (out of 49) for Years 4 and 8 maths and 13th for Years 4 and 8 science.' In science, our kids were equal to students in Germany, Italy, Lithuania and Sweden, which doesn't sound too bad at all.

But before you become too proud, there's another international test that seems to suggest that most people in

Australia may be too dumb to function in the modern world. That was the implication of the Adult Literacy and Life Skills Survey, conducted in 2006 on 8988 Australians aged 15 to 74. The test looked at four qualities: prose literacy; document literacy; numeracy; and problem solving. It was designed to check how many people displayed skills which are 'the minimum required for individuals to meet the complex demands of everyday life and work in the emerging knowledge-based economy'.

Here's the state and territory breakdown: In the Northern Territory, 72 per cent of people were assessed as having **less than adequate problem solving skills**; in Queensland, 70.8; in Victoria, 70.6; in New South Wales, 70.3; in South Australia, 69.6; in Tasmania 69.1 and in Canberra 54.5.

As the bureau describes the tests, **this is what 15.1 million Australians can do**: 'Tasks in this level typically require the respondent to make simple inferences, based on limited information stemming from a familiar context. Tasks in this level are rather concrete with a limited scope of reasoning.'

But this is what 10.6 million Australians cannot do: 'Some tasks in this level require the respondent to order several objects according to given criteria. Other tasks require the respondent to determine a sequence of actions/events or to construct a solution by taking non-transparent or multiple interdependent constraints into account. The reasoning process goes back and forth in a non-linear manner, requiring a good deal of self-regulation. At this level respondents often have to cope with multi-dimensional or ill-defined goals.'

The bureau's most disturbing discovery was that 59 per cent of Australians 'have difficulty with tasks such as locating information on a bottle of medicine about the maximum

number of days the medicine could be taken, or drawing a
line on a container indicating where one-third would be'.

The bureau notes: 'The ability to access and use health
information is **a fundamental skill** which allows people to make
informed decisions and helps them to maintain basic health
. . . Skill level 3 is regarded as the minimum required to allow
individuals to meet the complex demands of everyday life.
In 2006, [only] 41 per cent of adults were assessed as having
adequate or better health literacy skills, scoring at level 3 or
above. At this level, people could generally perform tasks such
as combining information in text and a graph to correctly
assess the safety of a product.'

The only good news is that we seem to be smarter than
Canada, where 31.6 per cent have 'adequate' problem solving
skills (to our 32.2 per cent). But we are dumber than Norway
(39.2 per cent) and Switzerland (33.8 per cent).

Now, hold on a minute. The bureau is telling us that two-
thirds of the people in Switzerland, one of the richest
countries on the planet, with no natural resources apart from
snow, do not have the problem solving skills to function in
modern life. Before we start beating up on ourselves, it may be
time for the testers to reassess their definition of 'adequate'.

WHAT AUSTRALIANS BELIEVE

In 2005, The Australian National University's Centre for Social Research published 'Australian Social Attitudes: A First Report'. Edited by Shaun Wilson, the report analysed the results of a mail questionnaire completed by 4270 adults. It was followed by a second report, 'Australian Social Attitudes 2: Citizenship, Work and Aspirations', in 2007, based on 3900 responses. These turned out to be the major opinions held by Australians:

To be 'truly Australian', it is 'fairly important' that you: 'speak English', 92 per cent agree; 'feel Australian', 91 per cent; 'have Australian citizenship', 89 per cent; 'respect Australia's political institutions and law', 89 per cent; 'be born in Australia', 58 per cent; 'be Christian', 36 per cent.

'The father should be as involved in the care of his children as the mother': 90 per cent agree.

'A woman should have the right to choose whether or not she has an abortion': 87 per cent agree.

'The gap between those with high incomes and those with low incomes is too large': 84 per cent agree.

'Generally speaking, Australia is a better country than most other countries': 83 per cent agree.

'When big businesses break the law they often go unpunished': 81 per cent agree.

'Media ownership in Australia is too concentrated among a few rich families': 81 per cent agree.

'There should be a law to protect all workers in Australia against unfair dismissal': 79 per cent agree.

'Large international companies are doing more and more damage to local businesses in Australia': 75 per cent agree.

'Immigrants make Australia open to new ideas and cultures': 74 per cent agree.

'People who receive welfare benefits should be under more obligation to work': 73 per cent agree.

'It is better for society if immigrant groups adapt and blend into the larger society': 71 per cent agree.

'Television violence encourages social violence': 71 per cent agree.

'The media should have less power': 70 per cent agree.

'Award wages are the best way of paying workers and setting conditions': 69 per cent agree.

'Unions should have less say in how wages and conditions are set': 52 per cent DISAGREE (with only 24 per cent agreeing).

Asked what makes a good citizen, more than half the sample identified these qualities as very important: 'Always vote in elections' (69 per cent); 'Always obey laws and regulations' (66 per cent); 'Never try to evade taxes' (61 per cent); and 'Keep watch on actions of government' (54 per cent).

'Immigrants are generally good for Australia's economy': 69 per cent agree.

'Australia should limit import of foreign products to protect the economy': 65 per cent agree.

Which institutions should be publicly owned: prisons, 67 per cent; Australia Post, 67 per cent; public transport, 63 per cent; electricity, 60 per cent; Telstra, 57 per cent.

'Commercial television is my daily source of news and information': 65 per cent (ABC and SBS, 41 per cent; radio, 63 per cent; newspapers, 40 per cent).

'Management and employees have good relations in my workplace': 62 per cent agree.

'Political parties do not give voters real policy choices': 62 per cent agree.

'The government doesn't care what people like me think': 61 per cent agree.

'Australia should pursue greater economic ties with Asia': 56 per cent agree.

'Overall, how satisfied are you with your job?': 47 per cent highly satisfied, 11 per cent highly dissatisfied.

'The death penalty should be the punishment for murder': 47 per cent agree, 33 per cent disagree.

'Australia's television should give preference to Australian films and programs': 46 per cent agree, 24 per cent disagree.

'The government should redistribute income from the better-off to those who are less well-off': 44 per cent agree, 30 per cent disagree.

'A preschool child is likely to suffer if the mother works': 44 per cent of men agree, 30 per cent disagree; 31 per cent of women agree, 45 per cent disagree.

'The number of immigrants allowed into Australia should be': decreased, 38 per cent; the same, 31 per cent; increased, 26 per cent.

'Smoking marijuana should not be a criminal offence': 32 per cent agree, 49 per cent disagree.

'If the government had a choice between reducing personal income taxes or increasing social spending on services like health and education, which do you think it should be?': Increase social spending, 47 per cent; lower taxes, 34 per cent; stay same as now, 19 per cent.

'Over the next ten years, the national priorities should be': Maintain a high level of economic growth, 53 per cent; a stable economy, 50 per cent; maintain order in the nation, 37 per cent; give people more say in important government decisions, 37 per cent; progress towards a less impersonal and more human society, 21 per cent; make sure this country has strong defence forces, 20 per cent. (Respondents were allowed two choices.)

Shown the statement **'Most of the time we can trust people in government to do what is right',** only 40 per cent of Australians agree. But in Japan, only 9 per cent agree. In Germany, it's 10 per cent, in France 22 per cent, in Britain 29 per cent and in the United States 31 per cent. The only nations that trust their governments more than we do are Denmark, Finland and Switzerland.

Asked about their fellow citizens, 58 per cent of Australians say other people can 'almost always' or 'usually' be **trusted**, while that is said by only 26 per cent of Japanese, and 46 per cent of Britons and Americans.

2

PECULIARLY OURS

SYMBOLS

Anthem: 'Advance Australia Fair' (*see* page 161) by Peter Dodds McCormick was written in 1878 and approved by referendum to replace 'God Save the Queen' in 1977.

Coat of arms: A shield divided into six states, supported by a red kangaroo and an emu, was declared in 1912.

Colours: Green and gold, declared in 1984.

Flags: The Blue Ensign displays one large white star and a five-star Southern Cross on a navy blue background with a British Union Jack in the top-left corner. It was chosen in 1901 from 32 823 entries in a design contest, and officially declared in 1953. The Aboriginal flag, a yellow sun on a horizontally divided background of black (the night sky) and red (the earth), was designed by Harold Thomas and officially included in the *Flags Act* in 1995. The Torres Strait Islander flag has two green bars, two black bars, one blue bar and a white star topped by a head-dress.

Flower: The golden wattle, *Acacia pycnantha*, declared in 1913.

Gemstone: The opal, declared in 1993.

Honours: The highest awarded by the Australian Government is the AC, the Companion of the Order of Australia (up to 25 are given each year). Next comes AO, Officer of the Order of Australia; AM, Member of the Order of Australia; and OAM, Medal of the Order of Australia.

Dish: Spaghetti bolognese (cooked most often at home and ordered most often when eating out).

Drink: At home, instant coffee; outside the house, cappuccino.

Tipple: With food, sauvignon blanc (Oyster Bay from New Zealand is the top-selling brand. It replaced Queen Adelaide chardonnay in 2009); without food, beer (Victoria Bitter).

Condiments: Tomato sauce (in 90 per cent of households); soy sauce (in 70 per cent of households).

Spreads: Vegemite; Nutella.

Fast foods: Pizza; hamburgers.

Footwear: Thongs.

Nuisance: Blowfly.

Salute: Waving the fly away.

Greeting: G'day.

Metaphor: The Magic Pudding.

In August of 2009, Prime Minister Kevin Rudd offered this analysis of an Opposition proposal on climate change: 'This is a rolled-gold, unreconstructed, Magic Pudding from Central Casting!' He thus became the latest in a long line of Australian politicians who have drawn upon the image of an endlessly renewable resource invented in 1918 by the artist Norman Lindsay. Lindsay described Albert the Pudding thus: 'The more you eats, the more you gets. **Cut and come again** is his name, and cut and come again is his nature.'

Rudd's predecessor, John Howard, referred to his Labor opponent in the 2004 election as 'Mr Magic Pudding himself'. Howard's predecessor, Paul Keating, accused his Liberal opponents of regarding Telstra as 'some sort of magic pudding, where you actually take a slice out of it and when you look at it, it's still there'. For politicians, Albert is the endlessly reusable metaphor.

VALUES

Bet on anything. Australians are gambling addicts, starting from the epidemic of 'chuck farthing' (two-up) reported by the *Sydney Gazette* in 1805. Every year we lose $15 billion on games of chance, which means that on average every adult throws away $1000 a year, mainly on poker machines, casinos, horse racing and lotteries (such as Lotto, scratchies and the pools). State governments gain 12 per cent of their revenue from taxes on gambling.

The cultural cringe. A belief, prevalent until the 1970s, that any work done by Australians would inevitably be inferior to the work of British and American people, and that we needed them to teach us how to be 'world class'.

The cultural strut. A belief, growing since the 1970s, that we have nothing to learn from other countries because Australians are the best in the world at sport, acting, directing, winemaking, modelling and music. (Since 2003 there has been a small revival in the cultural cringe, as Australians avoid their own dramas on television and their own movies at the cinema.)

Early adopting. Australians embrace new communications technology faster than the citizens of any other country. Colour television, the CD player, the VCR, the mobile phone, and the DVD player had all spread to more than half the nation's homes within eight years of their introduction. The only gadget that failed to seize our imagination was subscription TV (delivered by cable or satellite), which seems stuck at 28 per cent penetration—probably because we have too many other sources of amusement.

Fair go. It's what everyone is entitled to, but particularly the little Aussie battler. We don't believe there is a class structure.

There should be no such thing as inherited privilege in this country—unless it's my kids.

Laconic understatement. 'Not too bad' means 'excellent'. 'That'll do' means 'job well done'. 'You're not wrong' means 'I wholeheartedly agree'. 'Bit off colour' or 'not 100 per cent' means 'gravely ill'.

Loving to lose. There's a theory that Australia, founded by rejects from British society, is more inclined to celebrate failure than success, with a national holiday devoted to a military fiasco (Anzac Day), a hero hanged after bungling a bank robbery (Ned Kelly), an alternative anthem about a sheep thief who commits suicide ('Waltzing Matilda'), and a film industry that keeps making self-critical movies that nobody goes to see.

The Lucky Country. The title of a 1964 book by Donald Horne, who argued that Australians were taking the country's natural advantages for granted and should improve their national management. His ironic meaning is now lost, and the term is a boast about our blessings.

Mateship. Loyalty to friends, workmates and people of the same class, manifested particularly in the principle that you never dob. Reporting someone to the authorities, even when you know they are committing serious crimes, has been a no-no since convict days because, after all, whose side are you on?

Outback nostalgia. Since 85 per cent of Australians live within 50 kilometres of the sea, our self-image as a nation of bush battlers is a century out of date. Suburbanites identify with the outback by wearing Akubra hats and using overpowered four-wheel drives to take the kids to school, where bush ballads are still taught as Australian poetry. The mythology permeates everyday speech: 'bush telegraph' (rumours), 'bush lawyer' (untrained expert), 'bushwalking' (getting exercise in a forested area), 'bush medicine' (treatments known to Aboriginal people), 'go bush' (disappear), 'bush tucker' (edible native plants such as quandongs and lemon myrtle and edible animals such as kangaroo and crocodile), and 'What do you think this is—bush week?' (a mythical period when the usual social restraints do not apply).

Reconciliation. Most Australians welcomed the 2008 decision by Prime Minister Kevin Rudd to apologise to Aboriginal people for taking their land in the 18th and 19th centuries, and for taking their children in the 20th century (a policy of assimilation condemned in 'The Stolen Generations Report' issued in 1996 by the Human Rights and Equal Opportunity Commission). A minority of Australians believe governments have already done enough to relieve poverty and ill-health in Aboriginal communities and they should now be able to look after themselves.

Self-deprecating humour. Q: What's an Aussie man's idea of foreplay? A: Are you awake, love? Q: Why do Aussie men come so quickly? A: So they can get to the pub and tell their mates about it.

She'll be right. The phrase implies a laid-back approach to work and relationships, signifying calm optimism or complacent fatalism. The sentiment underlies other slogans such as 'No worries'; 'Don't get your knickers in a knot'; 'Settle down'; 'Get real'; 'Give it a rest'; and 'I'd rather be sailing'. John Howard expressed the notion during the 1999 election campaign when he said Australians wanted to be 'relaxed and comfortable'. After the events of 11 September 2001, this changed to 'alert but not alarmed'.

Tall poppy syndrome. A tendency to ridicule those who display arrogance about their wealth, fame or success. It often involves the recounting of scandals about politicians, entertainers and businesspeople—some of which may be true.

Wordplay. The creation of diminutives by adding '-ie' or '-o' or '-a', as in 'We thought we'd give the kiddies their Chrissie pressies by the barbie this year, so come round for brekkie and bring your cossie, a few tinnies and something to stop the mossies'. Or 'The journo reckons the garbo's off on compo because he went troppo'. Or 'Did you see that Kezza [Kerry Packer] met Chazza [Prince Charles] and they talked about Bazza [Barry McKenzie]?'

We also enjoy **reverse nicknames**—a red-haired person called Bluey, a dark-haired person called Snowy, a short person called Lofty. And rhyming slang: 'Have a captain at that' (Captain Cook = look); 'Let's go to the rubbidy' (rubbidy dub = pub); 'Me old china' (china plate = mate).

The yellow peril. Some Australians believe we should seek 'engagement with Asia', since we are geographically closer to China, Indonesia and Malaysia than we are to Britain or the United States, and we have embraced Thai, Chinese and Japanese influences in our cooking culture. Other Australians fear 'Asianisation' will mean immigrants who work harder than Australians and immigrants' children who beat local children at school and university. People of Asian background are less than 5 per cent of the population.

During the Noughties, the yellow peril was replaced by '**boat people panic**', as some Australians feared invasion by asylum seekers, and politicians debated how to be both tough and humane.

HOW WE SPEAK

Australia has 226 **languages**. After English, the most popular are Italian (spoken at home by 354 000 people), Greek (264 000), Cantonese (225 000) and Arabic (209 000).

Our version of English contains hundreds of expressions unfamiliar to Americans, Brits, Canadians, South Africans and New Zealanders. Derived from Aboriginal languages*, or from now-vanished English, Scottish or Irish dialects, or from jokes only we understand, they include:

'Ang on, or 'Ang about: wait a moment.

'Avago ya mug: give it a try, don't hold back.

Banana republic: what former treasurer Paul Keating thought Australia was in danger of becoming if we didn't fix our economy.

Barra: short for barramundi*, a fish native to northern waters.

Barrack: to cheer a team or player (the US equivalent is 'root', which has a different meaning here, so that 'root, root, root for the home team' sounds to us like an invitation to an orgy).

Battler: hard-working poor person.

Bindi-eye*: a painful thorn encountered by bare feet in summer grass.

Blind Freddy: the person who can immediately see the bleedin' obvious: 'Blind Freddy can tell he's a bludger.'

Bloke: a down-to-earth man; drinking beer and watching footy displays 'blokiness'.

Bludger: a lazy person who takes advantage of others.

Blue: an argument or fight, as in 'get in a blue' (but 'true blue' means 'honest' or 'fair dinkum').

Bodgie: in the 1950s, a flashy teenage boy with groomed hair (the self-confident politician Bob Hawke was called 'the silver bodgie'); the female equivalent is 'widgie'. Referring to an object, bodgie can mean 'fake' or 'poorly constructed'.

Bogan: an unfashionable working-class person. The term was popularised by the Melbourne schoolgirl character Kylie Mole in the TV series *The Comedy Company*.

Boofy: dumb and masculine, as in 'big boofy bloke', derived from a comic strip character called Boofhead. It's the opposite of poofy.

Buckley's chance: highly unlikely: 'You've got Buckley's of ever getting him to shout.'

Budgie: short for budgerigar*, a small colourful native bird (a tight swimming costume on a man is known as a '**budgie smuggler**'; Kylie Minogue is 'the singing budgie').

Cactus: defeated, in big trouble: 'If she finds out, you're cactus.'

Chuck a wobbly: go into a rage.

Chunder: vomit, spew, technicolour yawn, go the big spit, drive the porcelain bus.

Clayton's: a safe alternative, derived from Clayton's tonic, 'the drink you have when you're not having a drink'.

Coo-ee*: a cry to attract attention in the bush.

Corroboree*: a ritual gathering; the late 20th-century family habit of watching a movie on television at 8.30 pm every Sunday night was known as 'the national corroboree'.

Cot-case: ill, often mentally.

Crikey: 'Good heavens!'

Crook: sick or angry: 'Don't go crook on me', or 'I'm feeling crook today.'

Dag: an unfashionable person, derived from a term for the matted wool around a sheep's anus.

Daks: trousers.

Dead set: completely or honestly: 'Dead set, Mum, I'm dead set gonna finish it.'

Didgeridoo*: long hollow wooden tube that amplifies chanting.

Dog's breakfast: a mess, same as 'mad woman's breakfast', or 'mad woman's knitting'.

Donkey vote: a way of demonstrating ignorance or apathy that is only possible because of Australia's compulsory preferential system. A donkey voter unthinkingly numbers the candidates from the top of the card to the bottom.

Dorothy Dixer: a question you have asked someone to put to you because you already know the answer. The term, derived from a newspaper columnist who solved the romantic problems of her readers, is used most often in parliament, where political leaders eagerly respond to Dorothy Dixers from their own supporters.

Dreaming: Aboriginal legends, sometimes called 'alcheringa'.

Drongo: a boring fool, derived from the name of an unsuccessful Melbourne race horse in the 1920s; similar to 'nong', 'drip', 'dickhead', 'dropkick', 'galah' and 'silly nana'.

Drover's dog: the animal helped to move cattle across the outback, but now the term means 'any random individual'. Forced to hand over the Labor leadership to Bob Hawke in 1983, Bill Hayden said, 'I believe that a drover's dog could lead the Labor Party to victory, the way the country is and the way the opinion polls are showing up for the Labor Party.'

Duco: the shiny paintwork on a car.

Dunny: outdoor toilet, but 'bangs like a dunny door' is a synonym for promiscuity.

Fair enough: agreed, acceptable; often preceded by 'Goodo'.

Few bricks short of a load: stupid or mad; similar to 'not playing with a full deck', 'lights on but nobody's home', 'a few sandwiches short of a picnic' and 'some roos loose in the top paddock'.

Flake out: to have a rest, collapse, fall asleep.

Furphy: an implausible story, often about a famous person.

Gutful: enough.

Hoon: a noisy lair.

Jackaroo: a man who goes to work with horses, cattle or sheep on a country property; the female equivalent is a 'jillaroo'.

Koori: an Aboriginal person from southern New South Wales or Victoria; the Queensland equivalent is 'Murri', and the South Australian is 'Nunga'.

Kn'oath: definitely (short for 'fucken' oath').

Lair: a show-off; 'mug lair': a stupid show-off.

Larrikin: a person with a mischievous sense of humour.

Mate: friend; sometimes used to reassure a colleague before you betray him.

Mob: tribe or group of emotionally connected companions: 'Is he one of your mob?'

Mongrel: dishonest person, bastard.

Ocker: exaggeratedly Australian.

Onya: congratulations, short for 'good on you'.

Pea: the chosen one, the most likely winner: 'She's the pea.'

Pom: English person, derived from 'pomegranate', for the red cheeks of the new arrivals.

Poofter: homosexual (also 'willy woofter', 'queer', 'pillowbiter').

Ratbag: an eccentric person.

Rat's: don't care: 'I couldn't give a rat's (arse) about that.'

Recession we had to have: former treasurer Paul Keating's stern solution to an overheated economy in 1991, which caused voters to feel that he might not be the prime minister we had to have.

Ridgy-didge: genuine.

Rort: fake, cheat: 'He's rorting the voting figures.'

Sheila: woman.

Shonky: unreliable in business: 'He's a bit of a shonk.'

Shout: to buy a round of drinks.

Sickie: a day off work for illness (not necessarily genuine).

Skerrick: a tiny bit: 'There's not a skerrick of evidence for that.'

Skite: boast.

Slag off: to rubbish, criticise, insult, badmouth. In sport, it's called 'sledging'.

Smart alec: a pretentious person who shows off knowledge.

Sook: whinger.

Squatter: a rich farmer. Excessive rural influence on government indicates a 'squattocracy'.

Strine: the language we speak in Straya, as defined in the 1966 book *Let Stalk Strine* by Afferbeck Lauder (actually the linguist Alastair Morrison).

Stubbies: small bottles of beer or a small pair of shorts.

Swim between the flags: what you must do at a beach where the lifesavers have checked for rips and undertows. Also a metaphor for Australia's national identity, somewhere between Britain, America and Asia.

Trendie: an inner city person who frequents the latest restaurants, bars and fashion stores.

Veg out: to relax.

Uey: u-turn: 'Chuck a uey at the lights.'

Walkabout: to wander off, disappear: 'going walkabout' is supposedly a habit of Aboriginal people.

Wanker: a self-indulgent or pretentious or overly intellectual person.

Westie: a person from the working-class suburbs of Sydney or Melbourne.

Whadareya? A challenge, suggesting cowardice.

Whinger: complainer.

Wog: a non-English-speaking immigrant. The term has now been embraced by the children of immigrants, used in such satirical stage shows as *Wogs Out of Work*. Wog kids may call Anglo kids 'skips' (from 'Skippy' the bush kangaroo); originally an illness: 'I got a tummy wog.'

Woop-woop: a mythical village in the outback, beyond the black stump, in the never-never.

Wowser: a prude who tries to stop others having fun.

Write-off: destroyed, tired out: 'After the party, my car was a write-off and so was I.'

Wuss: a wimp, or nervous nellie.

Yabbie*: a small freshwater crayfish found in country ponds and dams; also called 'marron', 'red claw' and 'lobbie'.

Yobbo: an ocker slob.

Zed: the vanishing pronunciation of the last letter of the alphabet. Most Australians under the age of 20 prefer the American 'zee', thus endangering the old Aussie synonym for sleeping—'putting some zeds in the air'.

AUSTRALIANISMS

All over it like a seagull on a sick prawn.

All over the place like a wet dog on lino.

Better than a poke in the eye with a burnt stick.

Busier than . . . a one-armed taxi driver with crabs, a one-armed bill-poster in a stiff breeze, a one-armed bricklayer in Baghdad, a one-legged man in an arse-kicking competition.

Colder than a mother-in-law's kiss, a well-digger's arse, a witch's tit.

Couldn't . . . fight his way out of a wet paper bag, find a root in a brothel (with a fistful of fivers), organise a fart in a curry house, organise a pissup in a brewery, pour water out of a boot with instructions on the heel.

Couldn't sell . . . beer to a drover, ice-cream in hell.

Dry as . . . a dead dingo's donga, a pommy's bath towel.

Face like a dropped pie.

A few snags short of a barbie, bricks short of a load.

Finer than frog's hair.

Flash as a rat with a gold tooth.

Flat out like a lizard drinking.

Full as . . . a butcher's pup, a fat lady's gumboot, a Catholic school, a Corby boogie-board bag.

Going off like your nanna in Spotlight.

Gone like last week's pay.

Happy as a dog with two tails.

(The winner's) harder to pick than a broken nose.

Head like a chewed Mintie.

If he fell into a barrel full of tits he'd come up sucking his thumb.

(I'll be) off like . . . a bucket of prawns in the sun, a salami in the sun.

Missed it by a bee's dick.

Piss in my pocket but don't tell me it's raining.

Playing up like a secondhand whippersnipper.

Shoot through like a Bondi tram.

Silly as a bum full of Smarties.

Slick as snot on a door knob.

Smiling like a mother-in-law in a divorce court.

So bucktoothed, she could eat a watermelon through a barbed-wire fence.

So hungry . . . I could eat the arsehole out of a dead dingo, I could eat the crotch out of a low-flying duck.

Sticks to the road like shit to a blanket.

Sweating like a fat chick in lycra.

Tight as a shark's arse.

Up and down like a bride's nightie.

(I'd be) up that like a rat up a drainpipe.

Useless as . . . tits on a bull, a glass door on a dunny, a letterbox on a tombstone, a pork chop at a synagogue.

Vanished like a fart in a fan factory.

Welcome as a fart in a two-man sub.

Wouldn't shout in a shark attack.

Wouldn't turn up at his own funeral.

CATCHPHRASES

'Aussie Aussie Aussie, Oi Oi Oi' (TV, sporting events)

'Come on Aussie, come on.' (TV commercial, World Series Cricket)

'Cut and come again' (book, *The Magic Pudding*)

'A dingo ate my baby' (TV, based on the Azaria Chamberlain case)

'The drink you're having when you're not having a drink' (TV commercial for Clayton's tonic)

'Eight cents a day' (TV commercial, ABC)

'Happy little Vegemites' (radio commercial)

'How embarrassment' (TV, *Acropolis Now*)

'Hullo possums' (Stage and TV, Edna Everage)

'I'll rip yer bloody arms off' (TV, *The Aunty Jack Show*)

'I'll slip an extra shrimp on the Barbie' (TV, Paul Hogan tourism commercial)

'I Still Call Australia Home' (song, Peter Allen)

'It's noice, it's different, it's unusual' and 'Look at moyee' (TV, *Kath and Kim*)

'Just what this country needs: a cock in a frock on a rock' (film, *Priscilla, Queen of the Desert*)

'Lock it in' and 'Is that your final answer' (TV, Eddie McGuire on *Who Wants To Be A Millionaire*)

'Men and women of Australia' and 'Well may we say . . .' (speeches, Gough Whitlam)

'Not happy, Jan' (TV commercial for the *Yellow Pages*)

'Please explain' (TV, Pauline Hanson responding to the question 'Are you xenophobic?')

'Puck you, miss' and 'That's so random' (TV, Jonah and Ja'mie, *Summer Heights High*)

'Shaddup you face' (song by Joe Dolce)

'She goes, then she goes, she just goes . . .' (TV, Kylie Mole in *The Comedy Company*)

'So where the bloody hell are you?' (TV commercial for tourism)

'Spreading disease with the greatest of ease' (TV commercial for Mortein)

'Tell 'em they're dreamin' (film, *The Castle*)

'That'll do pig, that'll do' (film, *Babe*)

'That's not a knife, THAT'S a knife' (film, *Crocodile Dundee*)

'There was movement at the station' (poem, *Man From Snowy River*)

'There's nothing so lonesome morbid or drear as . . .' (song, 'Pub With No Beer')

'We don't need another hero' (theme song from *Mad Max: Beyond Thunderdome*)

'You're terrible, Muriel' (film, *Muriel's Wedding*)

THE SOUNDS OF US

Every year, the National Film and Sound Archive in Canberra asks the people of Australia to nominate recordings which demonstrate 'artistic excellence, historical relevance, technical or scientific achievement, and prominence in shaping **Australia's culture and identity**'.

The collection so far includes the radio serial 'Dad and Dave', the voice of the Antarctic explorer Ernest Shackleton, Percy Grainger playing his 'Country Gardens', Aboriginal songmaking, Gough Whitlam's 'Kerr's Cur' speech, Slim Dusty's 'Pub With No Beer'; the Aeroplane Jelly jingle; Johnny O'Keefe's 'She's My Baby'; a 1927 recording of 'Waltzing Matilda'; Nellie Melba's first commercial recording; Peter Dawson's 'Along The Road To Gundagai'; and 'We Have Survived' by No Fixed Address.

You can hear the recordings and offer your thoughts at www.nfsa.gov.au/whats_on/soundsofaustralia. Here are some suggestions for other sounds that represent the texture of this nation:

Rustic experiences: A creaky gate; lorikeets; a didgeridoo; an outdoor dunny door banging in the wind; driving over a cow grate; an windmill turning; rain on a corrugated iron roof; cows complaining as you try to make them get off the road; a flock of galahs coming in before sunset; cicadas drumming on a summer night; a car on a gravel road or crossing a wooden bridge; a screen door slamming; the popping of mangroves; geckos chattering on the ceiling; the splat of a cane toad on bitumen.

Urban experiences: The swipe of a credit card; the final siren of any AFL game; Pluto Pups being crisped to greasy excellence; the hiss of milk frothed by a cappuccino machine; garbos hurling bins around at 6 am; a waiter mispronouncing bruschetta (it's brusketta, not brooshetta); yobbos screaming 'F—off poofter' as their Holden Commodore sails past.

Suburban experiences: The *thump thump thump* of a creepy crawly stuck in the corner of a pool; the pattering of the first raindrops as a southerly buster comes through; the squeak of a Hills Hoist; the screech of a cockatoo before a storm; Magpies warbling; the whine of a mosquito on a steamy night; kookaburras; lifesavers megaphoning 'Get back between the flags'; a car door slamming and the patter of bare feet running across hot concrete at a petrol station; flying foxes fighting over fruit; a Victa mower turning your neighbour's grass into lawn at 8 o'clock on a Sunday morning; possums bounding across your roof under a midnight moon.

INVENTIONS

The Alexander technique
A method of relieving stress by improving posture, developed in Melbourne in the 1890s by Frederick Alexander.

Antivenenes for snake and spider bites
Since the 1950s, scientists at the Commonwealth Serum Laboratories have developed treatments for the bites of the taipan, the brown snake, the death adder, the seasnake, the redback spider and the sea wasp. In 1981, a team led by Struan Sutherland developed an antivenene for funnel-web spider bites.

Aspro
In 1915, George Nicholas, a Melbourne pharmacist, concocted a purer form of aspirin, originally made by the German company Bayer, and it became the world's favourite painkiller.

Bionic ear
In 1978, Graeme Clark of the Royal Victorian Eye and Ear Hospital in Melbourne developed a 'cochlear implant' that alleviates deafness by using a tiny radio to deliver sound directly to the brain.

Black box flight recorder
In 1954, David Warren of the Aeronautical Research Laboratories in Melbourne made a recording device for flight data and cockpit conversations that would be durable enough to survive a plane crash. The modern version is usually coloured orange.

Blue heelers
In 1890, the Australian cattle dog was perfected in Muswellbrook, New South Wales, after years of mixing Scotch

collie, dingo, dalmatian and kelpie. It is the only purpose-bred cattle dog in the world.

Boomerang
The name comes from the language of the Turuwal people, who lived just south of Sydney, but the inventor of the wooden club that returns when thrown is unknown.

Call girls
In 1891, Melbourne brothel owners set up the first system of ordering prostitutes by phone.

Cloud seeding
In 1947, the world's first man-made rainstorm soaked Bathurst, New South Wales, after dry ice was sprayed into clouds. The CSIRO Division of Cloud Physics continues to experiment with rainmaking using silver iodide particles around which ice crystals form.

Controlled crying
In the mid-1970s, Christopher Green of the Child Development Unit at the Royal Alexandra Hospital in Sydney introduced a procedure for creating regular sleep patterns in babies. It involves parents letting their children cry for increasingly longer periods before comforting them.

Counterfeit-proof money
In 1988, the Reserve Bank and the CSIRO introduced the world's first banknotes made of polymer plastic, lasting ten times longer than paper notes and almost impossible to forge. The Reserve's company, Securency, now makes money for 23 other countries, from Bangladesh to Zambia.

Dynamic Lifter
In 1971, Norman Jennings of Sydney demonstrated a method of making fertiliser pellets from chicken manure. It is now used around the world.

The Esky
In 1952, the Malley company introduced a portable drink cooler in the form of a steel box within a steel box (with ice between), changing in the 1970s to plastic and increasing the size.

The Fairlight Computer Music Instrument
In 1979, two Sydney engineers, Peter Vogel and Kim Ryrie, invented a music synthesiser that provided a lush backing for such 1980s performers as Peter Gabriel, Kate Bush, Duran Duran, Todd Rundgren and Stevie Wonder.

The feature film
In 1906, the world's first movie to run for more than an hour was *The Story of the Kelly Gang*, made in Victoria by Charles Tait.

Flight across the Pacific Ocean
In 1928, Charles Kingsford Smith was the first to fly from Oakland, California to Brisbane, Queensland.

Forensic lights
In 1989, Ron Warrender and Milutin Stoilovic of the Australian National University in Canberra developed a portable light that shows up invisible clues like blood stains, fingerprints and scribbled-over writing. The Polilight is used by police in 40 countries.

Freestyle swimming
From 1902, the stroke originally known as the Australian Crawl was introduced to the world in touring displays by the Sydney endurance swimmers Syd and Charles Cavill, and became the standard in international competitions.

Granny Smith apples
In 1868, Maria Ann Smith cultivated a long-lasting green apple in her garden in Eastwood, Sydney. Her children marketed it to the world.

Harmful effects of thalidomide
In 1961, William McBride of Sydney revealed that the morning sickness drug, thalidomide, could cause deformities in babies.

The Hawke olive harvester
In 2002, Tony Hawke, a farmer from Wauchope, New South Wales, designed a self-propelled machine that pulls olives off trees without bruising the fruit or damaging the branches. Built by his son Scott, the machine saves time and labour for Australia's booming olive oil industry.

The Hills Hoist
In 1946, Lance Hill welded pipes together in his shed in Adelaide and built a rotary clothesline able to be raised with a crank handle and strong enough for a child to swing on. Selling millions, it became the symbol of the suburban backyard.

The Humespun pipe
In 1910, brothers Walter and Ernest Hume of Melbourne patented a method of making strong pipes by spinning wet concrete inside a mould. By the 1920s, the method was used around the world.

Immunology
Since the Nobel Prize-winning work of Macfarlane Burnet in the 1940s, Australian medical researchers have led the world in helping the body's immune system fight disease. In 1991, Donald Metcalf of the Walter and Eliza Hall Institute in Melbourne identified 'colony stimulating factors' which encourage the body to make white blood cells.

The inflatable escape slide
In 1965, Jack Grant of Qantas invented a slide that helps passengers evacuate a crashed plane and turns into a life raft if the crash is in water.

The Interscan landing guidance system

In 1971, the CSIRO's Paul Wild perfected the ideas of Brian O'Keeffe for using microwave beams to scan the ground and let planes approach runways at a steeper angle.

The irrigation machine

In 1891, George Chaffey started pumping water from the Murray River onto land at Mildura, Victoria, using a massive steam engine he had designed. It turned Mildura into a fruit exporting centre.

Juvenile Court

In 1890, the world's first closed court designed to protect young defendants from 'criminal taint' was set up in Adelaide.

Kelpies

In the 1860s, the first purpose-built sheepdog was bred from Scottish prick-eared collies on Geralda Station near Forbes, New South Wales, and exported to the world after 1872, when it won the first Australian sheepdog trials.

Kiwi boot polish

In 1906, William Ramsay and Hamilton McKellan of Melbourne launched a shoe cream able to restore colour to faded leather. They named it for Ramsay's wife, who was a New Zealander, and by 1920 they had sold 30 million tins around the world. It is now owned by America's Sara Lee corporation.

Letter sorting machine

In 1930, the world's first letter sorter, designed by A.B. Corbett, was installed at the Sydney GPO.

Lithium

In 1949, John Cade, of Melbourne's Royal Park Psychiatric Hospital, started using lithium carbonate to settle the manic side of bipolar disorders.

Microsurgery
Since 1968, the Sydney surgeon Earl Owen has pioneered the use of powerful microscopes to allow the sewing together of separated body parts, especially fingers to hands and hands to arms.

Mulesing sheep
In 1937, the CSIRO recommended a technique developed by the South Australian grazier J.H.W. Mules to remove skin around a sheep's anus where blowflies might lay their eggs. The technique is regarded as cruel by animal liberation groups in the US.

The notepad
In 1902, J.A. Birchall, a stationer in Launceston, Tasmania, first marketed bundles of paper with the sheets gummed together along the top.

The pacemaker
In 1926, Crown Street Women's Hospital, Sydney, developed a machine to keep a baby's heart beating. It evolved into the battery-powered pacemaker made in the US in the 1950s. In the 1970s, the Australian company Telectronics developed a version that could last twenty years.

Pavlova
The weight of evidence now suggests that the recipe for this dessert of meringue, fruit and cream was first published in New Zealand, but it does seem to have been named (after a visiting ballerina) in 1935 by Bert Sachse, the chef at the Esplanade Hotel in Perth.

Pedal wireless
In 1925, Alfred Traeger, an Adelaide engineer, devised a method for rural people without electricity to power radio transmitters by using bicycle pedals attached to a small

generator. The invention allowed the Royal Flying Doctor Service to communicate with patients.

Penicillin

In 1940, Howard Florey, an Adelaide scientist working in Oxford, found a way to refine the antibiotic penicillin, then organised its mass production in America.

Permanent pleating

In 1957, the CSIRO released Si-ro-set, a process invented by Arthur Farnsworth for putting creases into wool garments.

Plastic lenses

In 1960, Noel Roscrow set up Scientific Optical Laboratories of Australia in Adelaide to make spectacle lenses out of a plastic called CR39. It became the world's biggest plastic lens maker, and also developed Perma-Gard scratch-resistant lens coating and multifocal lenses as an alternative to bifocals.

Preferential voting

Introduced in Queensland in 1892, and in federal elections from 1919, it enables voters to number candidates from most liked to least liked. Combined with compulsory voting (introduced in Queensland in 1915), it makes Australia the most participatory democracy in the world.

Prepaid mail

Before 1838, people paid when a letter was delivered. Then James Raymond, postmaster general of the colony of New South Wales, started selling stamped letter sheets at 15 pence a dozen. Two years later the London post office introduced the same idea in the form of a penny postage stamp.

Refrigeration

In 1851, James Harrison of Geelong, Victoria, first made artificial ice, using the principle that metal becomes cold when in contact with evaporating ether. His technology was

improved in 1861 by Eugene Nicholle of the Sydney Ice
Company, who used ammonia in his freezing plants, and was
funded by the merchant Thomas Sutcliffe Mort.

Splade

In 1943, William McArthur of Sydney designed a combination knife, fork and spoon marketed to the world in 1962 (as
Splayds) by Stokes Pty Ltd.

Stockwhip

Of unknown origin, the kangaroo-hide whip is more than two
metres long and controls sheep or cattle by making a cracking
noise when it moves faster than the speed of sound.

Stripper harvester

In 1843, near Adelaide, John Bull, a wheat farmer, and John
Ridley, a flour miller, developed a machine that pulled
the grains from stalks of wheat. It enabled Australia to start
exporting wheat to the world.

Stump-jump plough

In 1870, Robert Bowyer Smith of Kalkabury, South Australia,
broke a bolt on his plough and found it went over obstacles
more easily. His patented version is credited with opening up
Australia's scrub to wheat farming.

Surf reel

Designed in 1906 by Lyster Ormsby, captain of the Bondi
Lifesaving Club, and built by G.H. Olding, it involved a belt
which went around the lifesaver, attached to a rope which
went around a giant cotton-reel, by which the lifesaver could
be towed back to shore with the person rescued.

Tea tree oil

Originally an Aboriginal medicine, oil distilled from
melaleuca leaves can help to relieve cuts, skin infections
and acne.

Test-tube babies

Since 1973, Monash University researchers Alan Trounsen, Linda Mohr and Carl Wood have been developing techniques for in-vitro fertilisation. They helped the birth of the world's first test-tube twins in 1983, and the first frozen embryo baby in 1984.

Toilet with dual flush

In 1980, Bruce Thompson, research and development manager with the Caroma company, redesigned the traditional cistern and toilet bowl to allow for two ways of flushing—11 litres for big jobs and 5.5 litres for small jobs. It can save 32 000 litres of water a year per household.

Totalisator

In 1913, George Julius of Sydney perfected a kind of computer (with wheels, cogs and weights) that automatically recorded bets, displayed odds and calculated winnings to help gambling on horse races. It was bought by racetracks around the world.

Ultrasound

In 1961, George Kossoff and David Robinson of the Commonwealth Acoustic Laboratory in Sydney developed a device for scanning human organs using ultrasonic waves.

Ute

In 1933, Lewis Brandt, chief engineer for Ford in Geelong, Victoria, designed a 'utility vehicle' that combined the seating comfort of a car with the carrying capacity of a small flatbed truck.

Victa mower

In 1952, Mervyn Victor Richardson, a Sydney mechanic, developed a lightweight two-stroke petrol lawnmower, which made his Victa company the biggest mower maker in the world. Slogan: 'Turn grass into lawn'.

Votes for women
South Australia was the second place in the world, after New Zealand, to let women vote in a general election: in 1894. Women voted for the federal government in 1902.

Wine cask
In 1965, Tom Angove of the Angoves wine company in Renmark, South Australia, patented the 'bag in a box' method of packaging and dispensing wine.

Wollemi Pines
In 1994, a park ranger in the Blue Mountains, west of Sydney, stumbled upon a stand of odd-looking conifers that turned out to be the last survivors of the world's oldest plants, unchanged for 200 million years. The Sydney Botanic Gardens Trust managed to breed from the 100 trees in the wild, and now Wollemi Pine seedlings are sold around the world.

Woomera
A breakthrough in weapons technology made more than 10 000 years ago, the woomera, or throwing stick, is a wooden lever that increases the speed and distance a spear will travel. The word comes from the Dharug language used around Sydney Harbour. Now also the name of a rocket testing range in the South Australian desert.

Zinc cream
In 1940, the Adelaide branch of Faulding Pharmaceuticals introduced tubes of white zinc oxide cream to block the sun's ultraviolet light and prevent skin cancers. Then, in 1999, Terry Turney, a CSIRO scientist, developed a transparent form of zinc cream.

THE MOST . . .

Liked people*

1 **Hugh Jackman**

2 **Andrew Denton**

3 **Jennifer Hawkins**

4 **Ernie Dingo**

5 **Dave Hughes**

6 **Magda Szubanski**

7 **Glenn Robbins**

8 **Hamish Blake**

9 **John Clarke**

10 **Shane Bourne**

*Every six months the research organisation Audience Development Australia shows pictures of 600 personalities to a sample of 2000 viewers in Brisbane, Sydney and Melbourne, and asks how they feel about the ones they recognise. The personalities above were most recognised and liked at the end of 2008.

Prescribed medicines

1 **amoxicillin** (antibiotic)

2 **paracetamol** (pain relief, e.g. Panadol)

3 **cephalexin** (antibiotic)

4 **atorvastatin** (anti-cholesterol, e.g. Lipitor)

5 **salbutamol** (anti-asthma, e.g. Ventolin)

6 **diazepam** (tranquilliser, e.g. Valium)

7 **temazepam** (sleeping pill, e.g. Normison)

8 **flu virus vaccine**

9 **levonorgestrel/ethinyloestradiol** (contraceptive pill)

10 **Metformin** (type 2 diabetes treatment)

Tallest buildings

Q1, Gold Coast (323 metres); **Sydney Tower** (305 metres); **Eureka Tower**, Melbourne (297 metres); **120 Collins Street**, Melbourne (262 metres); **Chifley Tower**, Sydney (240 metres).

Tallest mountains

Kosciusko (2230 metres above sea level); **Townsend** (2210 metres).

Note: Everest in Asia is 8848 metres

Highest temperature

53.1°C recorded at Cloncurry, Queensland, on 16 January 1889.

Lowest temperature

-23.0°C at Charlotte Pass, New South Wales, on 18 June, 1994.

Top rainfall

Happy Valley, north Queensland, with **4436 millilitres** a year; Australia's average is 465 millilitres, the lowest in the world.

Biggest deserts

Great Victoria in Western Australia and South Australia (348 750 square kilometres, or 4.5 per cent of Australia); **Great Sandy** in Western Australia (267 250 square kilometres or 3.5 per cent).

Note: Sahara in Africa is 9 065 000 square kilometres

Highest prices paid for Australian paintings

Brett Whiteley's '**The Olgas for Ernest Giles**' $3.48 million

John Brack's '**The Old Time**' $3.36 million

John Brack's '**The Bar**' $2.88 million

Brett Whiteley's '**Opera House**' $2.8 million

Clifford Possum Tjapaltjarri's **Warlugulong** $2.40 million

Frederick McCubbin's **Bush Idyll** $2.31 million

The highest price paid for a **painting by a woman** was $1.06 million in 2007 for Emily Kame Kngwarreye's **Earth's Creation**.

Biggest sites

The Big Banana at Coffs Harbour, NSW; **Trout** at Adaminaby, NSW; **Prawn** at Ballina, NSW; **Cheese** at Bega, NSW; **Merino** at Goulburn, NSW; **Ram** at Wagin, WA; **Crocodile** at Wyndham, WA; **Lobster** at Kingston, SA; **Orange** at Berri, SA; **Ned Kelly** at Glenrowan, VIC; **Penguin** at Penguin, VIC; **Truck** at Dysart, QLD; **Peanut** at Kingaroy, QLD; **Pineapple** at Nambour, QLD; **Guitar** at Tamworth, NSW.

Richest people

- **Anthony Pratt** of Melbourne, age 51, who inherited $4.3 billion in 2009 from his father Richard, 'the cardboard box king', who made his fortune from packaging and investments (Visy Industries).

- **Frank Lowy** of Sydney, 80, worth $4.2 billion from shopping centres and investments (Westfield).

- **Harry Triguboff** of Sydney, 78, worth $3.7 billion from property development (Meriton).

- **Gina Rinehart** of Perth, 57, worth $3.5 billion from iron ore royalties.

- **Clive Palmer** of the Gold Coast, 57, worth $3.4 billion from iron ore mining.

- **James Packer** of Sydney, 43, worth $3 billion from casinos, television, publishing and investments.

- **John Gandel** of Melbourne, 76, worth $2.7 billion from shopping centre developments.

- **Andrew Forrest** of Perth, 49, worth $2.4 billion from iron ore (Fortescue Metals).

Source: *BRW* magazine, 2009

WORLD RECORDS

Australia is the planet's **largest net exporter** of coal, accounting for 29 per cent of coal exports in the world.

The youngest person to **sail solo** around the world is David Griffiths Dicks, who was eighteen when he returned to Fremantle, Western Australia, on 16 November 1996, after 264 days, 16 hours and 49 minutes.

The **oldest continuous circus** in the western world was founded in Launceston in 1852 by Joseph Ashton and is still touring rural Australia with his descendants.

The **highest fee per minute** paid to an actor was US$3.7 million for Nicole Kidman's four-minute commercial for Chanel No. 5 in December 2003.

The **most golf holes** in a day (401) were played by Ian Colston at Bendigo Golf Club, Victoria, on 27 November 1971.

The **heaviest crab** (*Pseudocarcinus gigas*), weighing up to 14 kilograms, is found in Bass Strait near Tasmania.

The **heaviest aircraft ever pulled by a person** was a Boeing 747, weighing 187 tonnes, which was pulled 91 metres in 1 minute 27.7 seconds on 15 October 1997 by David Huxley in Sydney.

The **largest electorate** in the world is Kalgoorlie in Western Australia, which covers 2.6 million square kilometres and stretches 2250 kilometres north to south.

The **largest oyster** (*Ostrea hyotis*), weighing up to 3 kilograms, is found along the Great Barrier Reef in Queensland (which is the world's longest coral reef).

The **largest opal**, weighing 5.27 kilograms, was found at Coober Pedy, South Australia, in 1990.

The **largest wooden building** is Woolloomooloo Bay Wharf, Sydney, built in 1912.

The **largest deposit of iron ore** was discovered in 1952 in Western Australia by Lang Hancock, creating extreme wealth for him, and later his wife Rose and his daughter Gina Rinehart.

The **biggest gathering of Elvis Impersonators** involved 147 participants singing 'Love Me Tender' at the Elvis Festival in Parkes, New South Wales, in January 2007.

The **oldest person to graduate from a university** was Allan Stewart who received a Bachelor of Laws degree aged 91 years and 214 days, from the University of New England in October 2006.

The **longest cricket marathon** is 66 hours 16 minutes and was achieved by Raymond Terrace District Cricket Club at the King Park Sports Complex, Raymond Terrace, New South Wales, in January 2009.

The **fastest time to shear a single merino lamb** is 53.88 seconds by Australia's Dwayne Black on the set of 'Zheng Da Zong Yi—Guinness World Records Special' in Beijing, China, in September 2007.

The **fastest 50-metre human wheelbarrow race** was run by Josh McCormack (16) and Arjuna Benson (15), who took 14.87 seconds at Carey Baptist Grammar School, Melbourne, in September 2008.

The **largest underwater dance class** was held in October 2008 when 74 scuba divers danced simultaneously for ten minutes at the bottom of the pool at Sydney's Olympic Park Aquatic Centre.

The **largest espresso machine**, measuring 1.83 m × 0.54 m × 0.56 m, was built by AMANTI and displayed in September 2007 at the Fine Food 2007 exhibition in Sydney.

The **heaviest set of concrete blocks** broken over a person lying on a bed of nails was 16 blocks weighing 532.3 kg, broken over Neil Hardy at Vikings Auditorium, Erindale, Canberra, in February 2008.

The **most rugby tackles** made in one hour was 4130, done by students from Scots College, Sydney, in March, 2007.

The **longest train** ever assembled, stretching 7.35 kilometres, took 682 iron ore cars 275 kilometres from BHP's Newman mines to Port Hedland, Western Australia, on 21 June 2001.

The **longest bill** belongs to the Australian pelican, averaging 40 centimetres.

The **longest school lesson** lasted 54 hours, when Murry Burrows taught biology to 26 students at Laidley State High School, Queensland, from 15 to 17 April 2003.

The **longest tattooing session** lasted for 43 hours 50 minutes, achieved by Stephen Grady and Melanie Grieveson at the Twin City Tattoo And Body Piercing, Wodonga, Victoria, from 26 to 28 August 2006.

The **largest truffle** outside France, weighing 1 kilogram, was cultivated at Manjimup, Western Australia, in June 2005.

The **longest earthworm** (*Megascolides australis*), stretching up to 4 metres, is found in Gippsland, Victoria.

The **fastest speed on water** was 511.11 kilometres per hour, achieved by Ken Warby driving the jet-powered hydroplane *Spirit of Australia* on Blowering Dam Lake, New South Wales, on 8 October 1978.

Source: *Guinness World Records*

ICONS: PHYSICAL

They like us, they really like us. It's a pity, then, that we don't seem to like ourselves much. In 2009, the 'United Nation's Human Development Report' rated Australia as having the second best **'quality of life'** in the world (with Norway number one, the US 13 and Britain 21).

Clearly our campaigns, from 'Slip another shrimp on the barbie' to 'Where the bloody hell are you?' have worked. This revelation came as small consolation to local tourism officials pondering 2007 survey data which suggested that, if cost were no object, Australia is pretty much **the *last* place Australians would like to visit**. The Travel Research Centre, in a report to the Department of Industry, Tourism and Resources, said: 'Australians are searching for holidays that offer a significant contrast to everyday life . . . It is the prospect of a temporary "new life" that motivates them . . . Travel within Australia does not currently offer the experiences and gratifications sought from a holiday. Some Australians are currently resentful of the poor value for money travelling domestically offers . . . Not only is Australia not different, but it has a high degree of perceived homogeneity.'

The authors concluded there is 'a major long-term task to refresh Australia, especially in the eyes of younger consumers'.

Here's a list of must-sees within this continent that will change your mind about staying home . . .

The Blue Mountains, west of Sydney
Bondi Beach, Sydney
Broken Hill, NSW
Coober Pedy opal mines, SA
Cradle Mountain National Park, TAS

Daintree Rainforest National Park, north QLD

Dandenong Ranges, north of Melbourne

Federation Square, Melbourne

Flinders Ranges, SA

Fraser Island, north-east of Brisbane

Ghan Railway, 2979 kilometres or 47 hours between Darwin and Adelaide

Great Barrier Reef, 2000 kilometres along QLD coast

Harbour Bridge, Sydney

Indian-Pacific Railway, 4352 kilometres or 67 hours between Sydney and Perth

Jenolan Caves, west of Sydney

Kakadu National Park, and the Aboriginal rock art at Nourlangie, NT

Kings Canyon, Watarrka National Park, NT

Lord Howe Island, 700 kilometres north-east of Sydney

Margaret River wine region, WA

Melbourne Cricket Ground (also used for football), VIC

Monkey Mia, and the dolphins of Shark Bay, WA

National Gallery of Australia, Canberra

Ningaloo coral reef, off WA

Opera House, Sydney

Parliament House, Canberra

Phillip Island, to view the penguin parade, south of VIC

Port Arthur, TAS

South-west Karri forests, WA

Twelve Apostles, rock formations off the Great Ocean Road, VIC

Uluru (Ayers Rock) and **Kata Tjuta** (the Olgas), NT

ICONS: CULTURAL

Aboriginal art
A craze started in the 1970s when art dealers discovered the dot paintings of the Pintupi and Luritja people who live at Papunya, 250 kilometres west of Alice Springs, and persuaded them to make more portable creations by using acrylic paints on canvas. The big names are Clifford Possum Tjapaltjarri, who painted vast topographical 'maps' containing dreaming stories, Emily Kngwarreye, who painted the wildflowers and waterholes of the Red Centre, and Rover Thomas, who painted animal stories from the Great Sandy Desert of Western Australia.

Aeroplane Jelly
Coloured sugar and gelatine crystals first sold in 1927 and immortalised by a radio jingle in which a five-year-old girl sang 'I like it for dinner, I like it for tea', because 'a little each day is a good recipe'.

Akubra hats
The best use for the rabbit plague introduced into Australia in 1859. Tasmania's Benjamin Dunkerly turned skins into hats from 1872, naming them after an Aboriginal word for head covering. They're often worn with Drizabones, large oilskin coats designed to cover both horse and rider in a rainstorm.

ANZACs
Originally the acronym for the Australia and New Zealand Army Corps, who landed at Gallipoli in Turkey in 1915 as part of an unsuccessful British plan to stop Turkey's support

for Germany in World War I. The word now refers to all
servicemen who join the Anzac Day march on 25 April, and
has connotations of bravery, loyalty and persistence. Anzac
biscuits are made of golden syrup, desiccated coconut, rolled
oats, flour, butter and sugar.

Arnott's biscuits
We were upset in 1991 when the American Campbell's
company took over the bakery founded in Newcastle in 1865,
but we keep eating the Tim Tams, Iced VoVos, Adora Cream
Wafers, Saos, Nice, Jatz and Milk Arrowroots.

The Ashes
The prize for victory in cricket tests between England and
Australia. The first time we beat England on English soil
(1882), the London *Sporting Times* newspaper said English
cricket had died and 'the body will be cremated and sent to
Australia'. A burnt bail was placed in an urn and given to the
Australian team.

Aunty
The Australian Broadcasting Corporation is the government-
funded radio, television and web network. Aunty ABC is
regarded by some as too artsy-fartsy and lefty-intellectual, and by
others as pandering excessively to vulgar tastes, but it is valued
for its independence from commercial and political pressures.

Aunty Jack
Played by comedian Grahame Bond, she was the full-bodied
trans-gendered bike-riding hero of an ABC comedy series that
started in 1972 and generated the hit song 'Farewell Aunty
Jack', a catchphrase 'I'll rip yer bloody arms off' and a more
successful spin-off series *The Norman Gunston Show*.

Backyard
That patch of lawn behind the suburban bungalow where Australians enjoy their barbie, their Hills Hoist and, when they get a pay rise, their swimming pool.

Ben Ean Moselle
The semi-sweet white wine that started Australians on the road to sophistication in the 1960s. Made in Mildura from muscat, gordo and sultana grapes, it offered women an alternative to shandies (beer and lemonade) and sold at the rate of seven million bottles a year by the mid-1970s. The Ben Ean fad was replaced in the 1980s by the chardonnay fad.

Blinky Bill
A cartoon koala created in 1933 by Dorothy Wall in her book *Blinky Bill The Quaint Little Australian* and turned into a TV series in the 1970s.

Blue singlet
Until the 1970s, this was the standard garb of labourers, usually worn with shorts called stubbies.

Cherry Ripe
Chocolate-coated confection of coconut and cherries introduced in 1924 by MacRobertson's (now owned by Cadbury).

Chesty Bond
A comic strip hero introduced in 1939 to promote Bonds singlets, of which Australians had bought 300 million by the year 2000. In 2009, Pacific Brands retrenched 1800 workers and shifted Bonds singlet production to China.

Cleo
Launched in 1972, and soon selling 200 000 copies a month, it was the first Australian women's magazine to publish nude male centrefolds and to specialise in advice on how to achieve an orgasm.

Dad and Dave
Rural characters from an 1899 book called *On Our Selection* by Steele Rudd (real name Arthur Hoey Davis). Dave is dumb, Dad is cunning and Dave's wife Mabel is sweet.

Edna Everage
The sharp-tongued housewife from Moonee Ponds, Melbourne, created in 1955 by Barry Humphries. She has become an international superstar.

Grange Hermitage
Australia's greatest (and most expensive) red wine, created in 1951 by Adelaide wine maker Max Schubert using shiraz grapes with a little cabernet sauvignon. In the 1990s Grange became such a threat to the French wine industry that it made Penfold's remove the word 'hermitage' from the label.

The Greek Café
From the 1920s, Greek families spread through the country towns of this nation, opening eateries with names like Olympic, Paragon, and Acropolis. They deliberately didn't serve Greek food—unless you count 'Mixed Grill'—because we weren't ready for it. But in the 1930s, Zacharia Simos took a chance and brought a pastrycook from Athens to his Paragon tea rooms in Katoomba. In addition to scones and meat pies, they started offering the nut and honey pastries baklava and kataifi. The Paragon flourishes today as a monument to Australia's Greek heritage.

Norman Gunston

The Wollongong dork created for *The Aunty Jack Show* by actor Garry McDonald. Throughout the late 1970s Gunston managed to host his own successful tonight show whereon he sang, danced and conducted bizarre interviews with unsuspecting celebrities. A comeback attempt in 1993 ended when McDonald had a nervous breakdown.

Holden cars

The 'all-Australian car' designed by America's General Motors and first built here in 1948. Most nostalgia attaches to the Kingswood in the 1970s and the Commodore in the 1990s.

Barry Jones

A Melbourne schoolteacher with a photographic memory who won a fortune in prizes on the TV quiz show *Pick-a-Box* in the 1960s and became Minister for Science in the Hawke Labor government in the 1980s. He symbolises the lovable geek whose ideas are not necessarily practical.

Kath and Kim

The suburban mother and daughter from the ABC's hit sitcom are the Edna Everages of the 21st century. They introduced the catchphrases 'Look at moyee' and 'It's noice, it's different, it's unusual'.

Ned Kelly

A horse thief, bank robber, bushranger and murderer who operated in Victoria's Glenrowan area in the 1870s. He became a legend because he politicised his crimes as part of a struggle between poor Irish peasants and rich English landlords. He was hanged in Melbourne on 11 November

1880. Sidney Nolan's paintings of him in a rectangular black helmet hang in the National Gallery in Canberra.

Kokoda
Some call it a trail and some a track, but this 96-kilometre stretch of mountainous jungle in eastern Papua New Guinea has become a place of pilgrimage for Australians wishing to commemorate the 600 young soldiers who died in 1942 pushing back an attempted Japanese invasion.

Lamington
A cube of sponge coated with chocolate and dipped in dried coconut, symbolic of what our grandmothers used to make for afternoon tea. It falls into a category of 'nostalgia foods' that also includes the Neenish tart (a coracle of thick pastry filled with a dollop of jam and fake cream and topped with a yin and yang of vanilla icing and chocolate icing); the chocolate crackle (rice bubbles, copha and chocolate, sold at school fetes); the vanilla slice (custard between rectangles of crisp pastry, known in Melbourne as 'the snot block'); and the froggie cake (a small sponge with fake cream and green icing, popular in South Australia).

The loud shirt
In the mid-1980s, Dare Jennings, founder of the Mambo line of surf clothing, commissioned a group of cartoonists to design Hawaiian shirts that would be uniquely Australian. The result was a set of garish parodies of Australian stereotypes. The biggest sellers were 'The Beer Tree' and 'Aussie Jesus' by Reg Mombassa.

Louie the Fly
A dark character created in 1957 by Bryce Courtenay for Mortein fly spray commercials. He apparently has the power to resurrect from the dead—or the spray doesn't work.

Ern Malley

A fictitious poet created in 1944 as a hoax by two real poets, Hal Stewart and James McAuley. They persuaded a literary magazine called *Angry Penguins* to publish Malley's series 'The Darkening Ecliptic'.

Barry McKenzie

The hero of a 1960s comic strip by Barry Humphries in London's *Private Eye* magazine, later made into two movies. The strip satirised how the British saw Australian tourists: as sex-obsessed beer addicts with fifty synonyms for vomiting.

Ginger Meggs

A red-haired larrikin kid in a newspaper comic strip created in 1921 by Jim Bancks.

The Melbourne Cup

Since 1861, the nation has stopped on the first Tuesday afternoon of November to learn which big horse can gallop fastest round the 3200-metre circuit at Flemington racecourse.

Phar Lap

A big New Zealand-born chestnut gelding who won the Melbourne Cup in 1930, and died suddenly after he started winning races in America. Jealous Americans were suspected of his murder; now it seems he was accidentally poisoned when his trainer Tommy Woodcock gave him an arsenic-based tonic. Phar Lap's stuffed skin is in the Melbourne Museum.

Roy and H.G.

Roy Slaven and H.G. Nelson are mythical sports com-mentators originally created for radio Triple J by the comedians John Doyle and Greig Pickhaver. They enlivened the television coverage of three Olympic Games and have hosted numerous variety shows.

Skippy

Between 1967 and 1969, a company called Fauna Productions made 91 episodes of a series about a kangaroo that could dial a phone, open a safe, handle the controls of a helicopter, play the piano, and communicate sophisticated concepts by a series of clicks. *Skippy the Bush Kangaroo* was a hit in 128 countries over the next 20 years, and left a generation of Australians reluctant to eat the meat of a creature that was clearly the dolphin of the outback, if not the marsupial messiah.

Snugglepot and Cuddlepie

Gumnut babies created in the 1920s by the children's book illustrator May Gibbs. These chubby elves were friendly with native animals and curious about human beings, but lived in fear of the Big Bad Banksia Men. Gibbs also wrote a newspaper comic strip in which she called them Bib and Bub.

Southerly buster

The east coast name for a wind that suddenly cools the city after a humid summer day, known in Perth as the Fremantle Doctor.

Vegemite

In 1922, a Melbourne food entrepreneur named Fred Walker commissioned a chemist named Cyril Callister to develop an edible product out of the yeast that was thrown away after the manufacture of beer. Callister came up with a salty black paste that was christened Vegemite (on the analogy of the British product Marmite) after a contest conducted in 1923. In 1935 The Fred Walker Cheese Company was taken over by America's Kraftco, but Australians continued to love the paste. In 2009, Kraft introduced a variant with cream cheese swirled through it. Outrage greeted the first name for the new product—iSnack2.0—and by year end Kraft was calling it Cheesybite.

Violet Crumble bar
A chocolate-coated honeycomb confection introduced in 1923 by Hoadley's of Melbourne, now owned by Nestlé.

R.M. Williams
Reginald Murray Williams started making saddles, boots, pants and jackets in the north of South Australia in 1934, and in the 1980s his durable garments became a fad with urbanites and tourists. In 1988, he set up the Stockman's Hall of Fame in Longreach, Queensland.

Wogs Out of Work
Satirical stage show launched in 1987 by Nick Giannopoulos, Simon Palomares and Mary Coustas. Gave a comic voice to the children of a million immigrants who had arrived since 1946, and generated the TV series *Acropolis Now* and the movie *The Wog Boy*.

CREATED THERE, EMBRACED HERE

ABBA
Australians bought more of this quartet's albums than any other country (apart from Sweden). We put them on the soundtrack of two hit movies—*Priscilla, Queen of the Desert* and *Muriel's Wedding*. And we formed a tribute band, Bjorn Again, which we exported back to the northern hemisphere. And 25 years after Abba broke up, we bought half a million copies of the DVD of the movie *Mamma Mia!*.

Bikini
Invented in 1946 by a Frenchman and named after an atoll where the first US atomic tests were conducted, it first appeared on Aussie beaches in the late 1940s and caused inspectors to escort ladies off the sand to prevent public offence. The first Australian-designed bikini, by Paula Stafford, went on sale at Surfers Paradise in 1952.

Cappuccino
Italians only drink it with breakfast, but Australians drink it all day, frothy or flattened into caffé latte.

Desperate Housewives
During 2005, one in seven Australians watched this dramedy every week, compared with one in 13 Americans. Its suburban glamour and black humour struck a chord in the most suburbanised nation on earth. By 2009, its ratings had declined as we embraced a homegrown slice of suburbia—*Packed to the Rafters*.

Nutella

The chocolate-hazelnut spread created by Pietro Ferrero in
Alba, Italy, in 1946 is Australia's second best-selling spread
(after Vegemite).

The Phantom

Invented by American Lee Falk in 1936, but barely remembered
in his homeland, the 'Ghost Who Walks', with his wolf Hero,
his horse Devil and his support team the pygmy Bandar, became
immortal here as a magazine and newspaper comic strip.

Pink

The rock singer and songwriter whose real name is Alecia
Moore is pretty successful in her homeland, America, but
since 2006 has sold more albums in Australia than any
other performer—800 000 of *I'm Not Dead* and 700 000 of
Funhouse. In 2009 she spent four months doing 58 concerts
here and touring our cities and towns with her husband, the
motorbike racer Carey Hart.

Poker machines

Invented in America in 1908, but redesigned by Sydney's Len
Ainsworth in the 1950s, slot machines were legalised for use
in clubs by the New South Wales government in 1956. Now
Australia has 180 000 of them—21 per cent of the world's
total—and we put through $80 billion a year, winning back
$70 billion.

Thongs

Australia must admit that New Zealand gave the world the
rubber sandal with the band between the first and second toe,
allegedly based on ancient Japanese footwear. The Kiwis call
them 'jandals', while the Americans call them 'flip-flops' (and

use the word 'thong' for what we call a 'g-string'). Our athletes rode a giant thong in the 2000 Olympics opening ceremony, and costume designer Lizzie Gardiner made a dress entirely of pink and orange thongs for Hugo Weaving in the 1994 film *Priscilla, Queen of the Desert*. Overpriced thongs are now called Havianas.

Weber portable barbecue
Introduced here in 1978 by American entrepreneur Ross McDonald, this pod-shaped miracle allowed apartment dwellers to join a fad once confined to the backyard.

MADE HERE, EMBRACED THERE

Bananas in Pyjamas
The giant yellow do-gooders of Cuddles Avenue, originally created for *Play School* in 1988, now do marketing magic for the ABC in sixty countries.

Fosters beer
Invented in Victoria in 1887, now bottled in nine countries and sold in 150, Fosters has its fan base in Britain, where they imagine it's Australia's top-selling beer (a title actually held by Victoria Bitter).

Kangaroo as a delicacy
Most Australians avoid eating kangaroo meat, possibly because of its associations with our TV friend Skippy, but it is consumed eagerly by the French and the Germans, who consider it a healthy meat with low fat, high protein and plenty of iron.

Neighbours
The Melbourne teen soap and its Sydney clone *Home and Away* are seen in fifty countries by people who envy our big houses, white teeth and sunny lifestyle.

Paddle Pop
Invented in 1953 by Edwin Street at the Corrimal Ice Works, south of Sydney, and now owned by the English company Unilever, the ice-block is a hit in eighteen countries, including Vietnam and China.

Soap starlets
Since the late 1980s pretty graduates of *Home and Away* and *Neighbours* have headed to Hollywood and attempted American

accents. Those who found work in films and TV include: Simon Baker (*The Mentalist*); Rose Byrne (*Damages*); Emily de Ravin (*Lost*); Melissa George (*Grey's Anatomy*); Stephanie Jacobsen (*The Sarah Connor Chronicles*); Ryan Kwanted (*True Blood*); Dichen Lachman (*Dollhouse*); Ben Lawson (*The Deep End*); Radha Mitchell (*Finding Neverland*); Poppy Montgomery (*Without A Trace*); Teresa Palmer (*Bedtime Stories*); Jesse Spencer (*House*), Yvonne Strahovski (*Chuck*); Rachael Taylor (*Transformers*); and Anna Torv (*Fringe*).

Speedos
First made in 1929 by Sydney's MacRae Knitting Mills, and best known for the men's tight 'budgie smugglers' introduced in 1961, they became the cossie of choice for all 52 countries competing in the swimming events of the Montreal Olympics in 1976. Now the company is American-owned.

Ugg boots
The sheepskin slippers developed in the 1960s to keep the feet of Sydney surfers warm are a fad with US entertainers. An American company claimed ownership of the name in 2003, but in January 2006 the Australian trademark regulator ruled that Ugg, or Ugh (short for ugly), was a generic name (like thongs) and could be used by anybody.

The Wiggles
Created in 1991 for an ABC pre-schooler's program, the singing comedians Greg, Murray, Anthony and Jeff in their colourful skivvies earn around $45 million a year by selling products in America and franchising their concept to non-English-speaking countries. In 2005, they were named 'Australian exporter of the year' for selling 17 million DVDs and videos. In 2006, founding member Greg Page was replaced by Sam Moran.

MYSTERIES

What happened to Azaria Chamberlain?

In 1980, a two-month-old girl disappeared from a tent
in a camping ground near Uluru. Her mother, Lindy
Chamberlain, said she was dragged away by a dingo. In 1982,
Mrs Chamberlain was convicted of the child's murder and
spent four years in gaol before being declared innocent.

Who put the dope in Schappelle Corby's bag?

In 2005, a 28-year-old Queensland woman, described as a
'beauty student', was arrested at Denpasar Airport in Bali after
customs officers found a four-kilogram package of cannabis in
her boogie-board bag. After trial, she was sentenced to twenty
years in gaol. She says she was the victim of an international
smuggling racket. Conspiracy theories flourish about
Australian airport baggage handlers, drug dealers and even
members of her family.

Where is the Tasmanian tiger?

The last known thylacine died in Hobart Zoo in 1936, but
Tasmanians occasionally report forest sightings of a wolf-like
creature with yellow fur and dark stripes on its back.

What happened to Harold Holt?

In December 1967, the prime minister disappeared while
swimming in rough seas at Cheviot Beach, south of Melbourne.
One entertaining theory held that he was picked up by a
Chinese submarine. Another held that Holt was depressed over
waning support for his commitment to the Vietnam War.

Who carved the Marree Man?

In 1988, a four-kilometre-long carving of an Aboriginal hunter
appeared in the desert sands of Lake Eyre South, 60 kilometres

from the town of Marree in South Australia. In order to create the landmark, the site must have been surveyed from space and the figure would have taken months to plough.

What killed Bogle and Chandler?
On New Year's Day, 1963, the bodies of Gilbert Bogle, a CSIRO scientist, and Margaret Chandler, the wife of another CSIRO scientist, were found on the banks of the Lane Cove River near Chatswood Golf Course in Sydney. No cause of death has been determined. There was speculation they were working on secret drug projects for the CIA.

Who was attacking the Family Court?
In 1980, Judge David Opas of the Family Court was shot dead at the front door of his Sydney home. In 1984, a bomb went off at the Family Court in Parramatta, Sydney, and later that year the wife of Family Court judge Ray Watson was killed by a bomb at their home. No one has been charged with these crimes.

Where did all the money go?
During the 1980s, Australians briefly abandoned their traditional scepticism about tall poppies and admired the entrepreneurs Alan Bond (then boss of Channel 9 and Castlemaine Tooheys brewery), Christopher Skase (the boss of Channel 7 and Mirage Resorts) and John Elliott (boss of Elders IXL food company and Carlton United brewery).

By the mid-1990s, Bond and Skase were bankrupt, accused of fraud and with debts in the billions. And by the early 2000s, Elliott, a Liberal Party president once touted as a potential prime minister, was bankrupt and under investigation by the National Crimes Authority.

Our faith in capitalism was also shaken by the collapse in 2001 of One.Tel, a communications company founded by

Jodee Rich with a $375 million investment from James Packer (son of Australia's richest man at the time) and $575 million from Lachlan Murdoch (the son of one of the world's richest men).

These collapses would surely be candidates for the title of Australia's biggest corporate fiasco, but they were overshadowed by the collapse of the insurance company HIH in 2001, with debts totalling $5.3 billion. CEO, Ray Williams, and a director, Rodney Adler, were sentenced to four years' gaol, and businessman Brad Cooper got eight years for bribing HIH staff. Economists like to say that money is never lost: it simply moves around. So where is it?

What caused the Offset Alpine fire?

On Christmas Eve, 1993, a rundown printing factory in Sydney, owned by a company called Offset Alpine, burned to the ground. As a result, many prominent people made a great deal of money and one young woman lost her life.

The company had been sold for $15 million in 1992 by the media mogul Kerry Packer to a consortium controlled by a stockbroker named Rene Rivkin, who had managed to insure it for $53.2 million. Rivkin had sold shares in the company to a number of people including the Governor-General Bill Hayden, the federal Labor politician and lobbyist Graham Richardson, the NSW Labor politician Eddie Obeid, the TV presenter Ray Martin, and the entrepreneurs Rodney Adler and Sean Howard. After the fire, their investments increased considerably in value.

Rivkin committed suicide in 2005. In 2009, Rivkin's former chauffeur Gordon Wood (also an investor in Offset Alpine) was convicted of murdering his former girlfriend Caroline Byrne by throwing her over a cliff. One theory about motive was that she had threatened to reveal something about the fire.

CREATURES WE LOVE

Bilby: Cuddly alternative to the Easter bunny, formerly called rabbit-eared bandicoot.

Budgerigar: Mini-parrot which became the world's most popular caged bird after the naturalist John Gould took a breeding pair back to England in 1840.

Dingo: Wolf-like wild dog brought here 7000 years ago by Aboriginal immigrants.

Echidna: Monotreme (using the same hole for excretion, sex and egg laying) with sharp spines, long snout and sticky tongue for catching insects; its image is on our five-cent coin.

Emu: Big flightless bird bred for meat, oil and feathers; less flavoursome than kangaroo, best eaten as mince or prosciutto.

Frill neck lizard: Harmless reptile that puffs out its collar to frighten predators.

Galah: A noisy parrot usually with a pink head and grey back.

Kangaroo: Hopping marsupial that carries its young in a pouch; its image is on our one-dollar coin; estimated population: 40 million; its meat is high in iron and low in fat.

Koala: Tree-climbing marsupial that eats eucalyptus leaves; currently endangered by the disease chlamydia; not edible.

Kookaburra: Kingfisher bird that comes in two types, the laughing jackass and the howling jackass.

Platypus: Furry duck-billed swimming mammal which is also a monotreme; its image is on our twenty-cent coin.

Wombat: Marsupial like a small furry pig that lives in a burrow.

CREATURES WE HATE

Bluebottle: Stinging nuisance that regularly invades beaches.

Bulldog ant: Most dangerous ant in the world, up to four centimetres long, with an occasionally fatal sting.

Cane toad: Imported nuisance that kills native animals in northern regions.

Crown of Thorns starfish: Slowly consuming the coral of the Great Barrier Reef.

Parasitic bush tick: World's most infectious blood feeder.

Saltwater crocodile: Up to eight metres long and found in swamps and rivers near the northern coastline; partial to foolish tourists.

Sea wasp (or box jellyfish): The sting can kill; most often found in northern tropical waters between October and May.

Sharks, especially the white pointer, the whaler and the tiger: they kill or injure an average of four swimmers a year.

Snakes, especially the taipan, the tiger and the death adder: each year they kill three people who don't receive antivenene in time.

Spiders, especially the funnel-web and the redback: deaths are now rare because of antivenene.

HEAVY DATES

New Year's Day: Public holiday on 1 January (or nearest weekday).

Australia Day: Public holiday on 26 January (or nearest weekday).

Chinese New Year: First week of February.

Sydney Gay and Lesbian Mardi Gras: Last weekend in February.

Labour Day: Public holiday on first Monday in March in Western Australia, second Monday in March in Victoria and Tasmania, first Monday in May in Queensland, and first Monday in October in New South Wales, the ACT and South Australia.

Daylight saving: Clocks go back one hour on the last Sunday in March, and forward one hour on the first Sunday in October (except in Queensland and Western Australia).

Good Friday and Easter Monday: Public holidays in late March or early April.

April Fool's Day: Hoaxes permitted till midday on 1 April.

Anzac Day: Public holiday on 25 April (or nearest weekday).

Mother's Day: Second Sunday in May.

Adelaide Cup Day: Public holiday on 16 May in South Australia.

Foundation Day: Public holiday on 6 June in Western Australia.

The Monarch's birthday: Public holiday on second Monday in June in all States except Western Australia, where it falls in September.

Father's Day: First Sunday in September.

Melbourne Cup Day: Public holiday in Victoria on the first Tuesday in November.

Remembrance Day: 11 November—a minute's silence at 11 am to mark the end of World War I.

Christmas Day: Public holiday on 25 December (or nearest weekday).

Boxing Day: Public holiday on 26 December, Sydney to Hobart Yacht Race begins.

Proclamation Day: Public holiday in South Australia on 27 December.

3

A POTTED HISTORY

OUR TIMELINE

40 million BC
The island we call Australia breaks free from a much bigger landmass, now known as Gondwana.

Before 50 000 BC
People arrive from the lands in the north and start spreading across the continent.

40 000 BC
Aboriginal people engrave animal images on rocks in the Olary region of South Australia, creating the world's **oldest known art**.

35 000 BC
The Aborigines reach Tasmania.

30 000 BC
A long cold spell kills off the 'mega fauna': giant wombats (*Diprotodon australis*), emus (*Genyornis newtoni*), goannas (*Megalania prisca*) and lions (*Thylacoleo carnifex*).

12 000 BC
Rising seas separate Tasmania from the mainland.

8000 BC
Rising seas separate New Guinea from the mainland.

1422
A **Chinese** fleet commanded by Admiral Hong Bau travels too far to the south and approaches the west coast of a big island that might be Australia.

1523-39
Portuguese sailors under the command of Cristavao de Mendonca map the south-west coastline of a big island they call 'Java le grand'.

1606
A Dutch ship, the *Duyfken*, lands on the northern tip of the island (a spot now called Weipa) but leaves quickly when a sailor is speared by the locals.

1616
A **Dutch** captain, Dirk Hartogh, lands on the west coast (now Shark Bay), nails a pewter plate to a tree, and names the place 'Eendrachtsland', after his ship.

1642
A **Dutch** captain, Abel Tasman, lands on an island south of the main continent and names it 'Van Diemen's Land', after the Governor of the Dutch East Indies.

1770
An **English** ship, HM *Bark Endeavour*, commanded by James Cook, maps the east coast of a continent the Dutch are calling 'Hollandia Nova'. Cook names the place 'New South Wales'.

1788 (26 January)
An English fleet of eleven ships, commanded by Arthur Phillip, delivers 770 convicted criminals plus

soldiers, sailors and administrators and establishes a penal colony in what Phillip calls 'Sydney Harbour'.

1789

Convicts perform Australia's first English play, *The Recruiting Officer*.

1790

Convict farmer James Ruse produces the first successful **wheat** crop. The Eora, Dharuk and Tharawal people, led by **Pemulwuy**, begin a resistance to the English colonists, burning crops and killing soldiers. (Pemulwuy is killed in 1802.)

1793

The first eight free settlers arrive in Sydney from London.

1794

Thomas Watling, a Scottish convict, completes Australia's first oil painting, 'A Direct North General View of Sydney Cove'.

1795

A German free settler, Phillip Schaffer, produces 90 gallons (410 litres) of white 'Rhinewine' at Parramatta. (The first **beer** is brewed by John Boston in 1796.)

1798

John Macarthur and Samuel Marsden bring merino sheep from South Africa and start a breeding program that ultimately makes **wool** our major export industry. The first platypus specimen sent to London is branded a hoax.

1803

The country's first newspaper, the *Sydney Gazette*, is published. The first **cricket** match is played between some free settlers and officers of the supply ship HMS *Calcutta* in Sydney's Hyde Park.

1804

Troops put down a rebellion by 300 convicts near Parramatta, with nine rioters shot and six leaders hanged. A new penal colony, later called '**Hobart**', is established on the southern island, now called 'Tasmania'.

1805

The *Sydney Gazette* reports an epidemic of **gambling** by 'chuck farthing', later called 'two-up'.

1808

A military coup, known as the 'Rum Rebellion', deposes Governor William Bligh in Sydney and the NSW Corps runs the town.

1809

Australia's first **post office** opens in the Sydney home of Isaac Nichols, who charges one shilling for each letter he passes on.

1810

Governor Lachlan Macquarie arrives to restore London rule. The first official **horse race**, clockwise around Hyde Park, is held in October.

1813

Explorers Blaxland, Lawson and Wentworth cross the Blue Mountains west of Sydney and open a path to the country's interior.

1814
Governor Macquarie begins an 'extravagant' building program and accepts a recommendation from the explorer Matthew Flinders that the continent be named 'Australia'.

1817
Australia's first **bank**, the Bank of New South Wales (now called Westpac) opens for business.

1819
The first **book** by an Australian, *A Statistical, Historical and Political Description of the Colony of New South Wales* by William Charles Wentworth, is published.

1825
A new penal colony, to be called '**Brisbane**', is established in the north to handle the most difficult convicts.

1829
The English establish the Swan River military base on the west coast, to be called '**Perth**'. Rugby **football** is first played—by soldiers at the Sydney barracks.

1831
The *Sydney Herald* is published (later called the *Sydney Morning Herald*).

1835
John Batman uses flour and blankets to 'buy' land from Aboriginal people at Port Phillip and establishes a settlement to be called '**Melbourne**'.

1836
Free settlers from Britain establish a community on the mid-southern coast of Australia, to be called '**Adelaide**'.

1838
Seven white settlers are executed for the **massacre** of 28 Aborigines at Myall Creek in northern New South Wales.

1843
The first elected Legislative Council shares power with the Governor of New South Wales.

1851
Victoria becomes a separate colony from New South Wales. Edward Hargraves announces he has found gold west of the Blue Mountains, starting a gold rush. The University of Sydney is founded with three lecturers and twenty-four students. A second gold rush begins in Victoria after a discovery near Ballarat, north-west of Melbourne. (Ultimately, the Victorian goldfields produce eight times as much gold as the New South Wales fields.) The first **Chinese** settlers arrive in search of gold and stay to run market gardens and restaurants.

1854
On 3 December, Victorian gold prospectors gather in the **Eureka Stockade** under their own Southern Cross flag, protesting police corruption and the cost of mining licences. Government troops put down

the rebellion; nearly 40 diggers and five troopers are killed and another hundred diggers are imprisoned.

1856
Melbourne stonemasons are given an **eight-hour working day**, pioneering improved conditions for other labourers. New South Wales beats Victoria in the first inter-colony cricket match, played in Melbourne.

1858
The population of the colonies reaches one million.

1859
The first **rabbits** are imported into Victoria by Thomas Austin, to make him 'feel at home'. They become a national plague.

1861
The first **Melbourne Cup** horse race is won by Archer.

1865
The first **stock exchange** opens in Melbourne (opens in Sydney in 1871). Scottish baker William Arnott opens a biscuit factory in Newcastle and goes on to make **Tim Tam**, Sao, Iced VoVo, Jatz and Milk Arrowroot biscuits.

1866
The New South Wales Colonial Secretary, Henry Parkes, greatly reduces state aid to religious schools.

1868
The final shipment of convicts, making a national total of 159 000, reaches Australia, landing in

Fremantle (transportation to the east coast ended in 1852). Maria Smith develops the Granny Smith long-lasting green **apple** in her garden at Eastwood, Sydney.

1870
The first **Australian Rules** football match is played in Melbourne between Scotch College and Melbourne Church of England Grammar School, with 40 players per side.

1872
Victoria introduces compulsory primary school education for all children (the other colonies follow by 1895). Fur cutter Benjamin Dunkerly starts using rabbit skins to make **Akubra** hats in Tasmania.

1877
Australia wins the first Test against England at the Melbourne Cricket Ground.

1879
The world's first officially declared **National Park** opens near Sutherland, south of Sydney. The first **recordings** of the human voice, on the Edison phonograph, are heard in Sydney, two years after Thomas Edison introduced the device in America. Athanasios Comino, from Kythera, opens the first of a chain of Greek fish and chip shops in Oxford Street, Sydney.

1880
Ned Kelly's **bushranger** gang is captured in Victoria and Kelly is

later hanged. The first telephone exchange opens in Melbourne, with 44 subscribers.

1882

Two hundred settlers from the Veneto region of north **Italy** form a commune near Lismore that sells fruit, wine and silk around Australia. It comes to be called 'New Italy'.

1883

A train service begins between Sydney and Melbourne.

1890

The Carlton and United Brewery in Melbourne starts making **Victoria Bitter**, destined to become our most popular beer.

1892

The Australian Labour Party (spelling changed to '**Labor**' in 1907) is formed in four cities by unionists disgruntled by the defeat of strikes in the shearing and shipping industries.

1894

Women get the **right to vote** in South Australian elections.

1895

A.B. 'Banjo' Paterson writes the words to '**Waltzing Matilda**' while staying at a property near Winton, Queensland.

1896

The first **moving pictures** are projected onto a screen by American magician Carl Hertz at the Tivoli Theatre, Melbourne. Marius Sestier,

an agent of the Lumiere Brothers in Paris, makes the first films in Sydney and Melbourne. Melbourne engineer Herbert Thomson builds Australia's first **car**: steam-powered (he goes out of business in 1912).

1897

A convention of politicians from the six colonies draw up a draft constitution for a united Australia. The first petrol-powered motor car, called 'The Hertel', is imported.

1899

Australia sends 16 000 troops to South Africa to help Britain in the **Boer War**: by 1902, 251 are killed and 267 are dead from disease.

1900

Referendums in every colony support **federation**.

1901

Australia becomes a Federation with six states. Edmund Barton becomes the prime minister in the first national election. The first federal parliament opens in Melbourne and passes an immigration restriction bill, which becomes known as the '**White Australia Policy**'. A parliamentary committee chooses, from 32 823 entries, a **flag** for Australia: six stars on a dark blue background with Britain's Union Jack in the top-left corner.

1904

An 1800-kilometre 'rabbit-proof fence' is completed in Western Australia.

1906

The world's first **surf lifesaving** club is formed at Bondi Beach in Sydney. The first full-length movie, *The Story of the Kelly Gang*, is made in Victoria.

1908

South Sydney wins the first **rugby league** premiership.

1911

The town of Palmerston on the north coast of the continent is renamed '**Darwin**' and it becomes the capital of the Northern Territory, which is controlled by the federal government.

1912

John Duigan flies the first successful Australian-designed and built aircraft near Kyneton in Victoria. The federal government sets up the **Commonwealth Bank** of Australia, intended to put community service ahead of greed, and it is based in Sydney.

1913

The national capital, **Canberra**, is officially named.

1914

On 4 August, Australia joins Britain in declaring **war** on Germany.

1915

On 25 April, the Australia and New Zealand Army Corps (ANZAC) launches an attack at **Gallipoli** in southern Turkey, but withdraws eight months later after 8500 are killed. The Queensland government makes voting in state elections compulsory (joined by the federal government in 1924). A Hawaiian, Duke Kahanamoku, introduces **surfboard riding** at Harbord Beach in Sydney.

1916

A referendum rejects conscription as a means of boosting the war effort.

1918

On 11 November, the Great War officially ends: 60 500 Australians were killed during its campaigns. The nation's **population** reaches five million.

1919

Ross and Keith Smith take 25 days to make the first **flight** from Britain to Australia.

1922

Queensland and Northern Territory Aerial Services (**QANTAS**) offers the first commercial flights.

1923

Vegemite, a black spread made from the waste products of beer manufacture, goes on sale in Victoria. The first **radio** station, 2SB (later renamed 2BL), starts broadcasting in Sydney.

1924

The American Kellogg's company starts making **Corn Flakes** in Sydney.

1927

The Australian Council of Trade Unions, based in Melbourne, is formed. The federal parliament moves to Canberra.

1928
The nation's first **traffic lights** are switched on in Melbourne. The Sanitarium Health Food Agency launches **Weet-Bix**.

1929
The **Speedo** swimming costume is first made by MacRae Knitting Mills in Sydney.

1932
The Sydney Harbour Bridge opens. Australia's favourite racehorse, **Phar Lap**, dies suddenly in America (poisoning suspected).

1933
Publisher Frank Packer launches the *Australian Women's Weekly*. Mick Adams (real name Joachim Tavlaidis) opens the first **milk bar** in Martin Place, Sydney, offering flavoured milk shakes for fourpence. Mario Faggion opens the first self-described **Italian restaurant**, Florentino, on the corner of Martin Place and Elizabeth Street.

1935
A meringue and cream dessert served at Perth's Esplanade Hotel is named the '**Pavlova**'. The **cane toad** is introduced in Queensland to eat cane beetles (but it eats everything else).

1936
The last known Thylacine (Tasmanian tiger) dies in Hobart Zoo (alleged

sightings are still sporadically reported).

1938
First Coca-Cola bottling plant opens in Waterloo in Sydney.

1939
On 3 September, Australia joins Britain in declaring **war** on Germany.

1941
Johnson + Johnson builds Australia's first **Band-Aid** factory in Sydney.

1942
On 19 February, Japanese planes bomb Darwin, killing 243.

1943
The first women (Enid Lyons and Dorothy Tangney) are elected to the federal parliament. The Commonwealth Serum Laboratories in Melbourne starts the world's first mass production of **antibiotics** (penicillin).

1944
Robert Menzies forms the Liberal Party.

1945
On 15 August, Japan surrenders, ending the war after the death of 39 500 Australians. Lance Hill builds a rotary clothes line in a shed in Glenunga, Adelaide (and goes on to mass produce it as **The Hills Hoist** in 1948).

1946
The federal government introduces a massive immigration program from

Europe, under the slogan 'populate or perish'. It adds three million to the population by 1980.

1948

The first **Holden** car goes on sale for £760.

1949

The federal Labor government sets up a spy agency, the Australian Security Intelligence Organisation (ASIO). The **Snowy Mountains Hydro-Electric Scheme** begins (one of the world's biggest engineering projects, employing 100 000 people and when completed in 1974 providing power and water to NSW and Victoria). The **Liberal Party**, in coalition with the Country Party (later renamed the National Party), is elected as the federal government, staying in power for 23 years.

1950

Australia sends troops to join America in fighting **North Korea** (339 Australians are killed by 1953).

1951

The NSW government introduces the world's first paid **sick leave** and paid long service leave. Frank McEnroe invents the **Chiko Roll** in Bendigo in Victoria. Near Adelaide, Max Schubert creates Penfold's **Grange Hermitage**, destined to become Australia's greatest red wine.

1952

Mervyn Victor Richardson invents the **Victa** rotary lawnmower in Concord,

Sydney. The Sydney company Malley introduces the Esky drink cooler.

1953

The first Gaggia **espresso machine** imported from Italy arrives at the University Coffee Shop in Lygon Street, Melbourne, launching a coffee craze across Australia's suburbs. Ted Street develops the **Paddle Pop** at Corrimal, near Sydney. Samuel Taylor Pty Ltd introduces **Mortein** fly spray in a pressure pack (first advertised on television by 'Louie The Fly' in 1957).

1955

Pub **drinking hours** in New South Wales are extended from 6 pm closing to 10 pm closing (Victoria follows in 1966). Barry Humphries first performs in Melbourne as **Edna Everage**. Ray Lawler's play, *Summer of the Seventeenth Doll*, about Queensland cane cutters, opens in Melbourne.

1956

On 16 September, Channel TCN 9 in Sydney makes the first **television** broadcast with Bruce Gyngell saying, 'Ladies and gentlemen, good evening and welcome to television.' In November, Melbourne hosts the Olympics. New South Wales legalises **poker machines** in clubs. 'Rock around the Clock' by Bill Haley, the first rock and roll single released on 45 rpm, sells 150 000 copies.

1957

The first Australian-made rock and roll record, 'You Hit the Wrong Note, Billy Goat' by Johnny O'Keefe, goes on sale; being the last 78 rpm single, it's a flop. Danish architect Jøern Utzon wins the competition to design the Sydney Opera House.

1958

Panadol (paracetamol) goes on sale, ultimately becoming Australia's largest-selling painkiller. **Qantas** launches the first around-the-world jet service, taking five days to go from Sydney to London via the United States. The first **Top 40** sales chart of recorded music singles is published by Sydney's 2UE. Slim Dusty's 'Pub With No Beer' becomes the first locally written and recorded single to reach number one.

1959

The population reaches ten million. South Coast, just south-east of Brisbane, renames itself the 'City of Gold Coast' and encourages high-rise developments near its main beach, **Surfers Paradise**. Aboriginal artist Albert Namatjira dies in gaol, while serving a six-month sentence for supplying alcohol to a relative.

1960

Australia's first **ten pin bowling** alley opens in Hurstville in Sydney. Fluoride is added into Sydney's water supply (other states follow within five years). Rolf Harris's 'Tie Me Kangaroo Down, Sport' is a hit in Britain.

1961

The **contraceptive pill** is approved for prescription by doctors. The

government-owned Totalisator Agency Board (**TAB**) provides the first legal off-course betting on horse races, initially in Melbourne.

1962

Australia's **Rod Laver** makes the tennis 'grand slam', becoming men's singles champion at Wimbledon, the US Open, the French Open and the Australian Open. The Commonwealth Serum Laboratories develops **snake bite** antivenene. Australia's first skyscraper, the 25-storey AMP Building on Sydney Harbour, is completed. Australian 'advisers' sent to join US troops to train South Vietnamese combatants in their war against **North Vietnam**.

1963

The 250 000th immigrant from Italy, Antonia Bellomarino, steps off the *Neptunia* in Melbourne and receives a set of silver cutlery.

1964

The Beatles tour Australia. Bernard 'Midget' Farrelly wins the world's first **surfing championships** at Manly Beach in Sydney. Rupert Murdoch launches a national daily newspaper, *The Australian*. The editors of the satire magazine *Oz*, Richard Neville, Richard Walsh and Martin Sharp, are sentenced to a six-month gaol term for obscenity (later overturned on appeal).

1965

The federal government introduces **conscription** for randomly selected

20-year-old males, to serve two years' national service in the army. The government sends more troops to **Vietnam** (496 are killed by 1972 when Australia withdraws). The Australian crime series *Homicide* starts on Channel 7 (and continues until 1975). In Adelaide, Roma Mitchell becomes Australia's first female judge.

1966

On 14 February, the **currency** changes from pounds, shillings and pence to dollars and cents (there were 12 pence in a shilling and 20 shillings in a pound). *Play School* starts on ABC television. Robert Menzies retires as prime minister after a record 16 years.

1967

In a referendum, 90 per cent of Australians vote to give full citizenship rights to **Aboriginal people**. Thomas Angove of South Australia develops the **wine cask** (a bladder in a box). In Melbourne, Ronald Ryan becomes the last person to be hanged in Australia. In December, Prime Minister **Harold Holt** disappears while swimming off Portsea in Victoria.

1968

Australia's first **heart transplant** operation at Sydney's St Vincent's Hospital is declared a success; the patient survives 45 days. The first Kentucky Fried Chicken store opens in Guildford in Sydney. Mail deliveries go from twice a day to once a day. In Sydney, police start using '**the breathalyser**' to test for drink-driving.

1969

South Australia legalises medically supervised **abortions** (followed by New South Wales and Victoria in 1972 and Queensland in 1986). Rallies against Australia's involvement in the Vietnam War are held in every state capital. In Sydney, the **rock musical** *Hair* features the first mass nude scene on stage.

1970

Germaine Greer publishes *The Female Eunuch*, arguing that women's liberation means a happier life for women and men. Adelaide holds its first Arts Festival.

1971

Queenslander Neville Bonner is appointed to fill a Liberal Party vacancy in the Senate, becoming the first Aboriginal member of parliament. The first **McDonald's** store opens in Yagoona in Sydney. Anti-apartheid protesters disrupt cricket and football matches when white South African teams are playing. The NSW Builders Labourers Federation imposes '**green bans**' to prevent development in Sydney's historic Rocks area.

1972

The first issue of *Cleo*, a magazine for young women, is launched, with a nude male centrefold. Tasmanians form the world's first 'Green' political party. The Labor Party, led by **Gough Whitlam**, is elected as the federal government on 2 December; within a year it ends conscription, removes the last vestiges of the White Australia Policy, makes university education free and lowers the voting age from 21 to 18.

1973
The **Sydney Opera House** opens after 16 years of construction. Patrick White becomes the first Australian to win the Nobel Prize for literature. The TV soap *Number 96* presents the first bare breasts and the first gay kiss on prime-time television. Australia's first legal **casino** opens at Wrest Point in Tasmania.

1974
American Express and BankCard introduce the first widely available **credit cards**. Inflation reaches 16 per cent. **Chardonnay** grapes are planted in commercial quantities by Leeuwin Estate vineyard in Margaret River, south of Perth. The federal government bans cigarette advertising on television. 'Advance Australia Fair' joins 'God Save the Queen' as an alternative national **anthem**. The first FM radio stations begin broadcasting in Sydney and Melbourne. Cyclone Tracy devastates Darwin.

1975
Colour TV sets go on sale. Melbourne philosopher Peter Singer publishes his book *Animal Liberation*, starting a worldwide movement. The measurement system changes from imperial (inches, ounces, gallons) to **metric** (centimetres, grams, litres):

there were 12 inches in a foot, 3 feet in a yard and 1760 yards in a mile; 16 ounces in a pound; eight pints in a gallon; and boiling point was 212 degrees Fahrenheit. *Picnic At Hanging Rock* leads a boom in Australian film-making.

1975
On 11 November, Governor-General **John Kerr** dismisses the Whitlam Government after the Liberal Opposition refuses to pass finance bills in the Senate. The Liberals, under Malcolm Fraser, win the ensuing election. The ABC launches radio 2JJ, the first non-commercial rock music station, in Sydney (it becomes **Triple J** and goes national in 1995).

1976
The *Family Law Act*, introduced by Labor to allow **no-fault divorce**, comes into force: there are 63 000 divorces in the first year (there were only 16 000 in 1975). The first '**boat people**' start arriving from Vietnam, welcomed by the federal government. South Australia decriminalises **homosexuality** (New South Wales follows in 1984).

1977
Former Liberal Party Senator Don Chipp forms the **Australian Democrat Party** as a middle path between Liberal and Labor, to 'keep the bastards honest'. In a referendum, Australians choose 'Advance Australia Fair' as their national anthem.

Queensland abolishes death duties (followed within three years by the other states and Canberra). Kerry Packer introduces World Series Cricket, aka '**the cricket circus**'.

1978
A team, led by Graeme Clark of Melbourne University, invents '**the bionic ear**', an implant that can defeat deafness. An American, Ross McDonald, introduces the Weber portable barbecue, allowing urban Australians to have barbies on the balcony.

1979
The first video cassette recorders (**VCR**) go on sale. Coffee consumption surpasses **tea** consumption. The federal government declares the Great **Barrier Reef** a national park to stop the Queensland Government allowing oil exploration there. Pam O'Neill becomes the first woman jockey to ride against men (at Moonee Valley in Melbourne).

1980
Azaria Chamberlain goes missing at Ayers Rock camping ground. Her mother, Lindy, is convicted of murder in 1982, but gets a full pardon in 1987. The first 'multicultural' TV network, SBS, begins broadcasting.

1981
The population reaches 15 million. The first automatic teller machines (**ATMs**) are installed outside banks. In Melbourne, Carl Wood and Christopher Chen develop a technology that produces the world's first test-tube twins (and in 1984, the first frozen embryo baby).

1983
Unemployment reaches 10 per cent. Labor under **Bob Hawke** wins the federal election, then intervenes to prevent the Tasmanian Government flooding the Franklin wilderness after a campaign by conservationists. The Australian dollar is floated on world markets as part of economic deregulation. A yacht owned by businessman Alan Bond takes the **America's Cup** from the Americans for the first time in 132 years. Cliff Young, aged 61, wins the Sydney to Melbourne walking marathon with a time of 5 days and 15 hours. Men At Work's song '**Down Under**' reaches number one in Britain and America. The first Australian death from AIDS is recorded at Melbourne's Prince Henry Hospital.

1984
The first compact discs (**CDs**) go on sale, ultimately replacing vinyl recordings. The federal government introduces a law banning discrimination on the grounds of sex.

1985
The soap *Neighbours* starts on Channel 7 (relaunched in 1986 on Channel 10). Australia's biggest media owner, Rupert Murdoch, becomes a US citizen. Ayers Rock is handed back

THE LITTLE BOOK OF AUSTRALIA

to its original owners and renamed Uluru.

1986

The first **mobile phone** goes on sale. *Crocodile Dundee* becomes the most successful film ever made in Australia.

1987

In October, a stock market crash ends the 1980s business boom.

1988

On 26 January, a crowd of 1.5 million gathers round Sydney Harbour to celebrate 200 years of white settlement. Sydney's Kay Cottee becomes the first woman to sail solo non-stop around the world.

1989

Queen Elizabeth II stops awarding imperial honours (**knighthoods**) to Australians.

1990

The first '**internet**' linkup is established between computers at the CSIRO and universities; it's called 'AARNet' (Australian Academic and Research Network).

1991

Treasurer **Paul Keating** replaces Bob Hawke as prime minister. Arnott's is taken over by the US company Campbells. Bananas in Pyjamas get their own show on ABC television.

1992

The High Court rules that Eddie Mabo and islanders from Torres Strait have '**native title**' to their land.

1994

The Native Title Bill becomes law, granting Aborigines ownership of traditional lands; the High Court rules in The Wik Case that native title **rights to land** can co-exist with the rights of pastoralists. The phone company, Telstra, starts changing all Australia's phone numbers from six or seven digits to eight digits.

1995

Pay TV (delivered by cable or satellite) begins. The Australian film industry enjoys a brief revival with the success of *Muriel's Wedding*, *The Adventures of Priscilla, Queen of the Desert* and *Babe*.

1996

The Liberals, under John Howard, win federal government from Labor. Tasmanian **Bob Brown** is elected as the first Green senator in federal parliament. After the massacre of 36 people in a random attack at Port Arthur in Tasmania, Prime Minister Howard introduces national anti-gun laws. The Northern Territory government legalises **euthanasia**, or 'the right to die' under medical supervision, but is overruled by federal parliament. During the year, 7492 '**boat people**', most seeking asylum, are placed in detention centres or on the island of Nauru.

1997

Conservative Queensland politician Pauline Hanson launches the One Nation Party, committed to cutting immigration and reducing assistance to Aboriginal people. Ted Matthews, the last surviving ANZAC who landed at Gallipoli in 1915, dies in Sydney at the age of 101. Michael Hutchence, lead singer of INXS, dies in Sydney aged 37, apparently after hanging himself.

1999

Australians vote 'No' (55 per cent of the vote) in a referendum on a **republic**; 67 per cent of Canberrans vote 'Yes'. Australian troops help East Timor gain independence from Indonesia.

2000

Sydney hosts the Olympics. The federal government introduces a **Goods and Services Tax** (GST) of 10 per cent, with fresh foods exempt.

2001

A Norwegian ship called *Tampa* rescues 438 would-be illegal immigrants when their boat from Indonesia sinks off the Western Australian coast; the Australian Navy takes the **boat people** to the island of Nauru and the federal government introduces a policy of 'mandatory detention of unauthorised arrivals' to deter people-smuggling. Ansett Airlines, founded in 1936, goes bankrupt.

2002

Eighty-eight Australians are among 202 people killed by car bombs placed by religious fundamentalists at Kuta Beach in **Bali**, Indonesia.

Macintosh launches a portable music player called the **iPod**, which becomes the most popular MP3 device in Australia (one million sold within two years).

2003

The population reaches 20 million. Australia joins America in invading **Iraq** to supposedly remove Saddam Hussein from power and his 'weapons of mass destruction'. The war is ongoing.

2004

Australia wins 17 gold medals, its highest total ever, at the Athens Olympics. John Howard wins government again, defeating Labor's Mark Latham, who retires from politics. Kim Beazley becomes Labor leader. After only six years on the market, Digital Video Discs (**DVDs**), which can store hours of bonus features, replace videotapes as the preferred way to watch movies at home.

2005

The federal government softens its policy on **asylum seekers** detained within Australia and releases several long-term detainees, but changes border laws to require all arriving asylum seekers to be processed offshore. It also changes industrial relations laws to make it easier for companies to dismiss employees.

2006

The economy booms because of high world prices for iron ore, coal and gold, but China and India begin to develop alternatives to buying from Australia.

2007

The federal government sends police, army, doctors and social workers into remote Aboriginal communities in the Northern Territory in an '**intervention**' designed to prevent child abuse. In the November election, John Howard loses government and his own seat. Labor's Kevin Rudd becomes prime minister.

2008

Kevin Rudd **apologises** to Aboriginal people for the way earlier generations treated them. Towards year end, the government tries to limit the effects on Australia of a global financial crisis by introducing a '**stimulus package**' that includes a cash handout to all citizens, to encourage spending. The iPhone goes on sale.

2009

In its budget, the Rudd government reveals that the stimulus package and the economic downturn has transformed a $20 billion surplus into a likely deficit of $50 billion. But **inflation** is at 3 per cent and **unemployment** is at 6 per cent, suggesting Australia is surviving the financial crisis better than most countries. The asylum seekers issue returns to haunt Kevin Rudd, as hundreds of boat people, mainly from Afghanistan and Sri Lanka, set off from Indonesia in hopes of settling in Australia.

2012

In a referendum, Australians vote to make the nation a **republic** and to abolish state governments. In a gesture of reconciliation, Prime Minister Julia Gillard appoints Peter Costello our first president.

4

IT'S BEEN SAID OF US . . .

AUSTRALIA'S MOST INSPIRING AND INFURIATING SPEECHES AND COMMENTARIES

Arthur Phillip, the first governor of the colony of New South Wales, warning the convict-settlers that he was about to get tough on **law and order**, 7 February 1788:

'Should I continue to pass by your enormity with an ill-judged and ill-bestowed lenity, the consequence would be, to preserve the peace and safety of the settlement, some of the more deserving of you must suffer with the rest, who might otherwise have shewn themselves orderly and useful members of our community. Therefore you have my sacred word of honour that whenever ye commit a fault, you shall be punished, and most severely. Lenity has been tried. To give it further trial would be vain. I am no stranger to the use you make of every indulgence. I speak of what comes under my particular observation: and again I add that a vigorous execution of the law (whatever it may cost my feeling) shall follow closely upon the heels of every offender.'

Robert Lyon, a teacher of Greek and English, at a public meeting at Guildford in Sydney in June 1833, discussing **how Aboriginal people might react to white settlers**:

'The law of nations will bear them out in repelling force by force. They did not go to the British Isles to make war upon you; but ye came from the British Isles to make war upon them. Ye are the invaders of their country, ye destroy the natural productions of the soil on which they live, ye devour their fish and their game, and ye drive them from the abodes of their ancestors . . . They have all along shown themselves ready to be reconciled, desirous to live in peace and amity with you, and even willing to be taught your manners, laws, and polity. Choose for yourselves. If ye determine upon a war of extermination, civilised nations will be mute with astonishment at the madness of a policy so uncalled for, so demoniacal. When your doom is passed, your own children, for whose sakes ye have invaded the country, will join with the disinherited offspring of those ye have slain to pour a flood of curses upon your memory.'

Richard Windeyer, a lawyer born in England, at the inaugural meeting of the Aborigines Protection Society in October 1838, **discussing the rights of Aboriginal people**:

'I cannot look upon the natives as the exclusive proprietors of the soil; nor can I entertain the ridiculous notion that we have no right to be here. I view colonisation on the basis of the broad principle laid down by the first and great Legislator in the command He issued to man "to multiply and replenish the Earth". The hunting propensities of the natives cause them to occupy a much larger portion of land than would be necessary to their support if it were under cultivation. And the only way to make them cultivate it is to deprive them of a considerable portion of it. The natives have no right to the land. The land, in fact, belongs to him who cultivates it first.'

Robert Lowe, a lawyer and member of the Legislative Council, at a protest meeting of 5000 people at Circular Quay on 11 June 1849, **demanding an end to the transportation of convicts** to provide cheap labour for landowners:

'The stately presence of our city, the beautiful waters of our harbour, are this day again polluted with the presence of that floating hell: a convict ship . . . I view this attempt to inflict the worst and most degrading slavery on the colony only as sequence of that oppressive tyranny which has confiscated the lands of the colony for the benefit of a class. That class has felt our power: they are not content to get the lands alone, which without labour are worthless, and therefore they must enrich themselves with slaves. As in America, oppression was the parent of independence, so it will be in this colony. And so, sure as the seed will grow into the plant, and the plant to the tree, in all times, and in all nations, so will injustice and tyranny ripen into rebellion, and rebellion into independence.'

Ned Kelly, a bushranger, explaining **why he killed policemen**, while holding hostages in a bank in Jerilderie in New South Wales on 10 February 1879:

'Certainly their wives and children are to be pitied, but they must remember those men came into the bush with the intention of scattering pieces of me and my brother all over the bush, and yet they know and acknowledge I have been wronged and my mother and four or five men lagged innocent. And is my brothers and sisters and my mother not to be pitied also, who has no alternative, only to put up with the brutal and cowardly conduct of a parcel of big, ugly, fat-necked, wombat-headed, big-bellied, magpie-legged, narrow-hipped, splay-footed sons of Irish bailiffs or English landlords which is better known as officers of Justice or Victorian Police, who some calls honest gentlemen . . . A Policeman is a disgrace to his country, not alone to the mother that suckled him. In the first place he is a rogue in his heart, but too cowardly to follow it up without having the Force to disguise it. Next, he is a traitor to his country, ancestors and religion, as they were all Catholics before the Saxons and Cranmore yoke held sway. Since then they were persecuted, massacred, thrown into martyrdom and tortured beyond the ideas of the present generation.'

Louisa Lawson, the publisher of *The Republican* newspaper (assisted by her son Henry), speaking at the inaugural meeting of the Dawn Club on 23 May 1889, **demanding the vote for women**:

'Pray why should one half of the world govern the other half? Is it just to first ensure the silence of the weaker half by depriving them of a citizen's status, and then inform them that by the laws of the stronger section this is the way they must act and this is the way the world may legally use them? Here in New South Wales every man may vote, let his character be bad, his judgement purchasable, and his intellect of the weakest, but an honourable and thoughtful and good woman may be laughed at by such men: they can carry what laws they please in spite of her. In divorce, men are protected from infidelity: not women. Wives may still be forced to live in the same house with a husband whom they hate and fear. Have women no need of a vote to protect them in these things and in the multitude of other interests affecting women and children? It remains for the women of Australia to say how long they will lag in the rear of the great onward march of liberal thought and women's advances. We have examples. Now we only need our own efforts.'

Henry Parkes, the premier of New South Wales, addressing the Federation Conference (he was called 'the father of federation' but died four years before it was achieved) in Melbourne on 6 February 1890, **urging the colonies to unite**:

'The crimson thread of kinship runs through us all. We know we represent a race for the purpose of settling new colonies which never had its equal on the face of the earth. We know, too, that conquering wild territory and planting civilised communities therein, is a far nobler, more immortalising achievement than conquest by feats of arms. Is there a man living in any part of Australasia who will say that it would be to the advantage of the world that we should remain disunited, with our animosities, border customs and all the frictions which our border customs tend to produce, till the end of time? I do not believe there is a sane man in the whole population who will say such a daringly absurd thing. As separate colonies we are of little consequence, but the potentate does not exist, the ruling authority in human affairs does not exist, who would lightly consider the decision of a united Australasia. We should grow at once: in a day, as it were: from a group of disunited communities into one solid, powerful, rich and widely respected power.'

Alfred Deakin, the first attorney-general of Australia (he was prime minister from 1903 to 1910), introducing the *Immigration Restriction Act* on 12 September 1901:

'It is not the bad qualities but the good qualities of these alien races that make them dangerous to us. It is their inexhaustible energy, their power of applying themselves to new tasks, their endurance and low standard of living that makes them such competitors. The effect of the contact of two peoples, such as our own and those constituting the alien races, is not to lift them up to our standard, but to drag our labouring population down to theirs . . . Members on both sides of the house and of all sections of all parties: those in office and those out of office: with the people behind them, are all united in the unalterable resolve that the Commonwealth of Australia shall mean a "white Australia", and that from now henceforward all alien elements within it shall be diminished. We are united in the resolve that this Commonwealth shall be established on the firm foundation of unity of race, so as to enable it to fulfil the promise of its founders, and enjoy to the fullest extent the charter of liberty under the Crown which we now cherish.'

John Monash, commander of Australian forces on the Western Front in World War I, explaining why we should celebrate **Anzac Day**, 25 April 1927:

'Anzac Day makes a special appeal to the hearts of all of us because of the special place it holds in our history, for it was on this day 12 years ago that the flower of Australia's youth flung itself against the beetling cliffs of Gallipoli and performed a memorable feat of arms which instantly welded the people of Australia into a nation, and proved to the entire world that our men and women were not unworthy of their sires. It is not too much that the people should pause for one day in the year to do homage to those men and to keep alive the spirit which animated that host of departed friends. But our duty does not end there. On us who have survived the stress of war and who have been safely restored to our homeland is laid the duty of helping to restore to Australia the mighty loss of that legion of men by devoting our lives and energies to that class of nation building in which they would have shared had they been spared. Remember, in war those who came out of battle had to carry on the fight in reduced numbers, so we who have been fortunate enough by the blessing of Providence to survive the war must now do our part, but not only our part; we must take up the burden of those we left behind. Only so can we worthily honour their memory.'

Jack Lang, the premier of New South Wales, trying to **open the Sydney Harbour Bridge** on 19 March 1932 (before Lang could cut the ribbon, Francis de Groot, a member of a right-wing group called The New Guard, rode up and slashed the ribbon with his sword, saying, 'On behalf of decent and loyal citizens of New South Wales, I now declare this bridge open'):

> 'Just as Sydney has completed the material bridge that will unite her people, so will Australia ultimately perfect the bridge which it commenced 30 years ago. The statesmen of that period set out to build a bridge of common understanding, that would serve the whole of the people of our great continent. The builders of that bridge, as the builders of this bridge, meet with disappointments, which make the task difficult sometimes: often delicate. But that bridge of understanding among the Australian people will yet be built, and will carry her on to that glorious destination which every man who loves our native land feels is in store for her.'

Robert Menzies, an opposition backbencher in the process of forming the Liberal Party, discussing **'the forgotten people'** in federal parliament on 22 May 1942:

> 'We don't have classes here as in England, and therefore the terms don't mean the same. It is necessary, therefore, that I should define what I mean when I use the expression "the middle class": those people who are constantly in danger of being ground between the upper and nether millstones of the false class war; the middle class who, properly regarded, represent the backbone of this country ... First it has a stake in the country. It has responsibility for homes: homes material, homes human, homes spiritual ... Second, the middle class, more than any other,

provides the intelligent ambition which is the motive power of human progress . . . Third, the middle class provides more than any other the intellectual life which marks us off from the beast; the life which finds room for literature, for the arts, for science, for medicine and the law . . . Individual enterprise must drive us forward. That doesn't mean that we are to return to the old and selfish notions of laissez-faire. The functions of the state will be more than merely keeping the ring within which the competitors will fight. Our social and industrial obligations will be increased. There will be more law, not less; more control, not less. But what really happens to us will depend on how many people we have who are of the great and sober and dynamic middle class: the strivers, the planners, the ambitious ones. We shall destroy them at our peril.'

Ben Chifley, prime minister from 1945 to 1949, explaining **the priorities of the Labor Party** on 12 June 1949:

'I try to think of the Labor movement, not as putting an extra sixpence into somebody's pocket, or making somebody prime minister or premier, but as a movement bringing something better to the people, better standards of living, greater happiness to the mass of the people. We have a great objective: the light on the hill: which we aim to reach by working for the betterment of mankind not only here but anywhere we may give a helping hand. If it were not for that, the Labor movement would not be worth fighting for. If the movement can make someone more comfortable, give to some father or mother a greater feeling of security for their children, a feeling that if a depression comes there will be work, that the government is striving its hardest to do its best, then the Labor movement will be completely justified.'

William McKell, premier of New South Wales from 1941 to 1947 and governor-general of Australia from 1947 to 1953, supporting Australia's 'populate or perish' **immigration program**, 22 January 1951:

'The great immigration project upon which we are now firmly embarked is undoubtedly one of the most constructive and notable events in the history of Australia. Immigration means the development of our resources, the strengthening of our security and defences and the rapid expansion of our population, while to hundreds of thousands of people in the United Kingdom and Europe, it means the opportunity to live a new life in Australia . . . In the nineteenth century period of rapid growth, a sense of "mateship", fair play, independence of spirit and self-reliance was engendered which forms a vital part of our tradition of nationhood. It is these qualities, which are among the best in the Australian character, that we must seek to pass on to the newcomers. By a wise handling of assimilation, our migrants will not only conform to our standards of citizenship, but will add their own contribution. There will be give and take. Assimilation will be a two way process, demanding much of both migrants and ourselves, and the result will be mutual enrichment. For the migrants are bringing to Australia not only the benefits of their knowledge and skills, but of their age-old cultures. The old and new should blend into a better and more varied community of people.'

Robert Menzies, prime minister of Australia from 1949 to 1966, welcoming **Queen Elizabeth II** to Australia, 18 February 1963:

'It is a proud thought for us to have you here, to remind ourselves that in this great structure of government which has evolved, you, if I may use the expression, are the living

and lovely centre of our enduring allegiance . . . You will
be seen in the next few weeks by hundreds of thousands,
and I hope by millions, of Australian subjects. This must
be to you now something that is almost a task. All I ask
you to remember in this country of yours is that every
man, woman and child who even sees you with a passing
glimpse as you go by will remember it, remember it with
joy, remember it in the words of the old seventeenth
century poet who wrote those famous words: "I did but see
her passing by, but yet I love her till I die."'

Arthur Calwell, leader of the opposition in federal parliament
from 1960 to 1967, opposing the government's decision to
send troops to **join America's forces in Vietnam**, 4 May 1965:

'We do not think it is a wise decision. We do not think
it is a timely decision. We do not think it will help the
fight against communism. On the contrary, we believe it
will harm that fight in the long term. We do not believe
it will promote the welfare of the people of Vietnam.
On the contrary, we believe it will prolong and deepen
the suffering of that unhappy people so that Australia's
very name may become a term of reproach among them
. . . And may I, through you, Mr Speaker, address this
message to the members of my own Party . . . I offer
you the probability that you will be traduced, that your
motives will be misrepresented, that your patriotism will be
impugned, that your courage will be called into question.
But I also offer you the sure and certain knowledge that
you will be vindicated; that generations to come will record
with gratitude that when a reckless government wilfully
endangered the security of this nation, the voice of the
Australian Labor Party was heard, strong and clear, on
the side of sanity and in the cause of humanity and in the
interests of Australia's security.'

Harold Holt, prime minister of Australia from 1966 to 1967, explaining Australia's **support for the Vietnam War** to US President Lyndon Baines Johnson, 30 June 1966:

'You have in us not merely an understanding friend but one staunch in the belief of the need for our presence with you in Vietnam. We are not there because of our friendship, we are there because, like you, we believe it is right to be there and, like you, we shall stay there as long as seems necessary to achieve the purposes of the South Vietnamese government and the purposes that we join in formulating and progressing together. And so, sir, in the lonelier and perhaps even disheartening moments which come to any national leader, I hope there will be a corner of your mind and heart which takes cheer from the fact that you have an admiring friend, a staunch friend that will be All The Way With LBJ.'

Robin Boyd, an architect and author of *The Australian Ugliness*, delivering the Boyer Lecture on ABC radio on 17 October 1967, with the theme **'creative man in a frontier society'**:

'Australia is divided: not into halves, but into two uneven sections: by a jagged vertical crack near the left end. Facing each other across it are two Australians who are as different and wary of each other as the Aborigine and Captain Cook. On the larger side is the modern Australian who believes in the long established, still popular anti-intellectual Australian values, who is convinced that the Australian state and rate of progress are satisfactory. On the other is the modern Australian who sees so many shortcomings in Australian social development that he is on the point of despair. The evolution from a sponge-like culture, absorbing everything useful that floats by, to a

crawling and finally free-ranging active culture happens
spontaneously and quite suddenly in a society, but only
when enough individuals consciously revolt against being
sponges . . . In the ever more crowded and competitive
world of the last third of the twentieth century the product
that the whole world is craving, and will reward most
highly whenever it finds it, is not our wool, and not even
our iron or bauxite or natural gas that lay here so long
waiting to be discovered. It is brains: not just acquisitive
brains and not just academic brains, but creative
brains, imaginative brains exercised to the edge of their
capacity: which is the sort of exercise that has been least
respected in our 180 years of development.'

Don Dunstan, premier of South Australia from 1967 to 1968
and from 1970 to 1979, moving for the **decriminalisation of
homosexuality**, 18 October 1972:

'It is certainly contrary to the majority public taste. But
surely that is not sufficient for us to say that, because most
of us do not regard this as something that is in any way
attractive but rather, repulsive, other people who view
the matter differently should have our views imposed
on them privately. The second suggestion is that there
is a necessity to help the people involved. The law as
it stands does not help the people involved: it does not
assist people to seek help. What is more, of course, one
must face the fact that the majority of people who are
homosexual do not regard homosexuality as a disease at
all, nor do they regard it as a condition to be cured. They
regard it as natural and normal. In those circumstances,
I do not believe that society has any right whatever to
trespass in this area. The purpose of the criminal law is
to protect persons from physical harm and from active

affront, and their property from harm also. Outside of
that area, I believe that the criminal law has no place at
all, and it is for the social influences of the community to
impose or induce or persuade the moral standards which
various sections of the community advocate, to establish
the moral standards which will be accepted by the
majority. The law is not a means of enforcing morality.'

Germaine Greer, touring Australia to promote her book,
The Female Eunuch, explaining the advantages of **women's
liberation**, March 1972:

'It's not at all alien to the Australian character. It's not at all
alien to Australian women, who are probably in some ways
less bullshit-ridden than other women. And they know
something about hard work, most of them, if only because
the garden is so hard to handle and it's got funnel webs in
it. Women's liberation is sexy, it's exciting, it's all kinds of
things, and it's here to stay. There is no turning it back. A
radicalised woman is not able to go back to the old one-two
hanky dropping routine. It's just too nauseating.'

Gough Whitlam, prime minister from 1972 to 1975, opening
Labor's election campaign, 13 November 1972:

'Men and women of Australia. The decision we will
make for our country on the second of December is
a choice between the past and the future, between
the habits and fears of the past, and the demands and
opportunities of the future. There are moments in
history when the whole fate and future of nations can be
decided by a single decision. For Australia, this is such
a time. It's time for a new team, a new program, a new
drive for equality of opportunities. It's time to create new
opportunities for Australians, time for a new vision of

what we can achieve in this generation for our nation and the region in which we live.'

Frank Sinatra, visiting singer, discusses **the media** while addressing his audience in Melbourne's Festival Hall, 8 July 1974 (the speech resulted in union members from all industries refusing to serve him for the remainder of his tour):

'We have a name in the States for their counterparts. They're called parasites, because they take and take and take and never give, absolutely never give. I don't care what you think about any press in the world. I say they're bums and they're always gonna be bums, every one of them. There are just a few exceptions to the rule: some good editorial writers who don't go out in the street and chase people round. It's the scandal man that really bugs you, drives you crazy. It's two-bit type work that they do. They're pimps, they're just crazy. And the broads who work in the press are the hookers of the press. Need I explain that to you? I might offer them a buck and a half, I'm not sure. I once gave a chick in Washington two dollars, and I overpaid her, I found out.'

Gough Whitlam, reacting to **the dismissal** of his government, 11 November 1975 (Labor lost the ensuing election):

'Ladies and gentlemen. Well may we say "God Save the Queen", because nothing will save the Governor-General. The proclamation which you have just heard read by the Governor-General's secretary was countersigned Malcolm Fraser, who will undoubtedly go down in Australian history from Remembrance Day 1975, as Kerr's cur. They won't silence the outskirts of Parliament House, even if the inside has been silenced for the next few weeks . . . Maintain your rage and enthusiasm through the campaign for the election now to be held and until polling day.'

Malcolm Fraser, prime minister from 1975 to 1983, addressing the Liberal Federal Council in July 1981, explains a **puritan philosophy** often attributed to him:

'Over the years, a quotation about what life was or wasn't meant to be like has often been talked about. Some people have said it represents my philosophy. I think that now is the time to let you into a secret. Only half of the quotation is ever quoted. In full, it says: "Life is not meant to be easy, my child; but take courage, it can be delightful".'

Paul Keating, prime minister from 1992 to 1996, launching the Year of the World's **Indigenous People**, at Redfern Park, Sydney, 10 December 1992:

'We took the traditional lands and smashed the traditional way of life. We brought the diseases. The alcohol. We committed the murders. We took the children from their mothers. We practised discrimination and exclusion. It was our ignorance and our prejudice. And our failure to imagine these things being done to us. With some noble exceptions, we failed to make the most basic human response and enter into their hearts and minds. We failed to ask: How would I feel if this were done to me? As a consequence, we failed to see that what we were doing degraded all of us . . . And if we have a sense of justice, as well as common sense, we will forge a new partnership. Ever so gradually, we are learning how to see Australia through Aboriginal eyes, beginning to see the wisdom contained in their epic story. I think we are beginning to see how much we owe the Indigenous Australians and how much we have lost by living so apart.'

Paul Keating, thanking election workers, 13 March 1993:

'Well, this is the sweetest victory of all. This is the victory for the true believers, the people who in difficult times have kept the faith. And to the Australian people going through hard times: it makes their act of faith all that much greater. It will be a long time before an Opposition party tries to divide this country again. It will be a long time before somebody tries to put one group of Australians over here and another group over there. The public of Australia are too decent and they are too conscientious and they are too interested in their country to wear those sorts of things. This I think has been very much a victory of Australian values, because it was Australian values on the line and the Liberal Party wanted to change Australia from the country it had become, a cooperative, decent, nice place to live where people have regard for one another . . . The people of Australia have taken us on trust and we'll return that trust and we'll care about those people out there, particularly the unemployed: we want to get them back to work. If we can't get them back to work immediately, as sure as hell we are going to look after them. We are not going to leave them in the lurch and we are going to put our hand out and we are going to pull them up behind us. And we are going to move along, this country is going to move along together.'

Poppy King, a businesswoman in the cosmetics industry, making the **case for a republic** at the Constitutional Convention in Canberra, 10 February 1998:

'If I had to explain to someone who had lost their memory that Australia's head of state was not actually Australian, I would feel utterly ridiculous. Take away the historical connection and the concept is absurd. No one is asking this nation to lose its collective memory nor to deny the importance of Britain in our history. What we are asking is to examine our future, to explore our values and reassess whether our current Constitution reflects those. It seems that a main argument against Australia becoming a republic is a fear of change, a desire to maintain the status quo rather than take the risk to develop something better. This desire concerns me greatly. Think of all the developments that have improved our lives, both tangibly and intangibly, that would have been lost had this attitude prevailed. Apathy is the enemy of progress and progress requires change. Many say the change to a republic is purely symbolic. If this is the case, let me pose this question with all due respect: why keep this particular symbol? You may say because of a special bond that we have with Britain, a bond that I am sure is a lot more meaningful to many of my elders than is possible for me to understand. I am here to listen to their views and I respect their passion, but I would like to ask them this: how do we explain to future generations that we place our faith in a citizen of a country other than our own? How do we explain to them that no matter how hard they work they can never be part of a monarchy? How do I explain to the children that I may have one day that they have been lucky enough to be born into a country where anything—anything—is possible except to become our head of state?'

Christopher Vogler, Hollywood screenwriter, discussing reaction to his book *The Writer's Journey—Mythic structures for storytellers and screenwriters*, 1998:

'Here and there in my travels I learned that some cultures are not entirely comfortable with the term "hero" to begin with. Australia and Germany are two cultures that seem slightly "herophobic".

'The Australians distrust appeals to heroic virtue because such concepts have been used to lure generations of young Australian males into fighting Britain's battles. Australians have their heroes, of course, but they tend to be unassuming and self-effacing and will remain reluctant for much longer than heroes in other cultures. Like most heroes, they resist calls to adventure but continue demurring and may never be comfortable with the hero mantle. In Australian culture it's unseemly to seek out leadership or the limelight, and anyone who does is a "tall poppy", quickly cut down. The most admirable hero is one who denies his heroic role as long as possible and who, like Mad Max, avoids accepting responsibility for anyone but himself.'

John Carroll, Professor of Sociology at La Trobe University in Melbourne, delivering the Deakin lecture on 12 May 2001, explaining **'the dreaming' of white Australians**:

'A people, to feel free to let their character virtues speak unimpeded, must be at ease in themselves. One of the leading symptoms of insecurity is a tendency to extremism, to fanaticism or fundamentalism. Peoples, like individuals, take flight into ideology, dogmatism and ranting when they feel under inner threat. It is a leading mark of Australia as a political culture to have always and without exception been sceptical of idealism, hostile to extremists, innately drawn to the moderate, the sensible, the unassuming. It points to a fundamental security of being. Special warmth has grown for kangaroo, koala, platypus and echidna that is more than the cuddly toy sort. The marsupials set a tone, in their way of being. In part it is their lack of aggression: except when cornered. The quiet way they go about negotiating their habitat has affinity with the way the people respond to bureaucratic controls. Calm resistance, except when cornered, has met the Australia Card,

Byzantine new tax systems and grand attempts to tidy up the constitution. The kookaburra reminds humans, prone to taking themselves seriously, that they are easy to laugh at. The totemism of Aboriginal tribal culture seems to be colonising the colonisers.'

John Howard, prime minister from 1996 to 2007, addressing the memorial service for victims of the **Bali bombings**, 17 October 2002:

'Our nation has been changed by this event. Perhaps we may not be so carefree as we have been in the past, but we will never lose our openness, our sense of adventure. The young of Australia will always travel. They will always reach out to the young of other nations. They will always be open, fun loving, decent men and women . . . It will take a long time for these foul deeds to be seen in any kind of context. They can never be excused. Australia has been affected very deeply, but the Australian spirit has not been broken. The Australian spirit will remain strong and free and open and tolerant. I know that is what all of those who lost their lives would have wanted and I know it is what all of those who grieve for them would want.'

Steve Vidler, actor (*Two Hands*) and director (*Blackrock*), explains why **Australians prefer American-made movies** to locally made ones, 11 April 2005:

'A contributing factor is the power of the national myth, both American and Australian. The American myth is the myth of their nation's settlement—that an individual with strong character can undertake a daunting task, overcome seemingly insurmountable odds, and become a great success. The Australian myth is also based on our nation's settlement—that we are convicts, delinquents, struggling outsiders, persecuted by an uncaring and alien authority, trapped in a harsh environment we did not choose and do not understand, that all survival and validation relies on not rising above or separating from the group, failure and suffering are our lot, and the best we can hope for is to survive. US films represent their myth with great commercial success. It is a very palatable story and one most audience members would prefer to see on a Friday night after a hard week at work. Australian films represent their myth equally well (*Gallipoli*, *Lantana* and *Shine* exemplify the dramatic version, *The Castle* and *Muriel's Wedding* the comic) but it is a far less palatable myth, and commercially far less saleable.

'Sometimes we try to appropriate the American myth for our stories. And a strange thing happens. Mostly Australian audiences will not believe it. Our myth (itself a fanciful construct with little relation to the realities of our history) is so deeply ingrained that we distrust any narrative that sees our environment as essentially benign, or triumphant success as the deserved outcome of our struggle. But we will willingly believe these things of Americans. Or of Australians pretending to be Americans. To this problem there is no solution but time. I believe future generations will outgrow the convict/bushranger/ Anzac myth, and embrace a new narrative that reflects more accurately the enormous potential that lies within them and within this blessed and beautiful country.'

Kevin Rudd, prime minister from 2007, addresses parliament on 13 February 2008 and **apologises to Aboriginal people**:

'Today we honour the Indigenous peoples of this land, the oldest continuing cultures in human history. We reflect on their past mistreatment. We reflect in particular on the mistreatment of those who were stolen generations—this blemished chapter in our nation's history. The time has now come for the nation to turn a new page in Australia's history by righting the wrongs of the past and so moving forward with confidence to the future.

'We apologise for the laws and policies of successive parliaments and governments that have inflicted profound grief, suffering and loss on these our fellow Australians. We apologise especially for the removal of Aboriginal and Torres Strait Islander children from their families, their communities and their country. For the pain, suffering and hurt of these stolen generations, their descendants and for their families left behind, we say sorry. To the mothers and the fathers, the brothers and the sisters, for the breaking up of families and communities, we say sorry. And for the indignity and degradation thus inflicted on a proud people and a proud culture, we say sorry.

'We the Parliament of Australia respectfully request that this apology be received in the spirit in which it is offered as part of the healing of the nation. For the future we take heart; resolving that this new page in the history of our great continent can now be written.

'We today take this first step by acknowledging the past and laying claim to a future that embraces all Australians. A future where this Parliament resolves that the injustices of the past must never, never happen again. A future where we harness the determination of all Australians, Indigenous and non-Indigenous, to close the gap that lies between us in life expectancy, educational achievement and economic opportunity. A future where we embrace the possibility of new solutions to enduring problems where old approaches have failed. A future based on mutual respect, mutual resolve and mutual responsibility. A future

where all Australians, whatever their origins, are truly equal
partners, with equal opportunities and with an equal stake
in shaping the next chapter in the history of this great
country, Australia.'

The Central Intelligence Agency reports on Australia in its *World
Factbook*, May, 2009:

'**Economy:** Australia has an enviable, strong economy with
a per capita GDP on par with the four dominant West
European economies. Emphasis on reforms, low inflation,
a housing market boom, and growing ties with China
have been key factors over the course of the economy's 17
solid years of expansion. Robust business and consumer
confidence and high export prices for raw materials and
agricultural products fueled the economy in recent years,
particularly in mining states. Drought, robust import
demand, and a strong currency pushed the trade deficit
up however, while infrastructure bottlenecks and a tight
labor market constrained growth in export volumes and
stoked inflation through mid-2008. The unwinding of the
yen-based carry trade in late 2008 has contributed to a
weakening of the Australian dollar. Tight global liquidity
has challenged Australia's banking sector, which relies
heavily on international wholesale markets for funding.
The economy remains relatively healthy despite falling
export commodity prices.

'**Environment** (current issues): Soil erosion from overgrazing,
industrial development, urbanization, and poor farming
practices; soil salinity rising due to the use of poor quality
water; desertification; clearing for agricultural purposes
threatens the natural habitat of many unique animal and
plant species; the Great Barrier Reef off the northeast
coast, the largest coral reef in the world, is threatened

by increased shipping and its popularity as a tourist site; limited natural fresh water resources.

'Geography: World's smallest continent but sixth-largest country; population concentrated along the eastern and southeastern coasts; the invigorating sea breeze known as the "Fremantle Doctor" affects the city of Perth on the west coast and is one of the most consistent winds in the world.

'Manpower available for military service: Males age 16–49: 4 999 988, females age 16–49: 4 870 043 (2008 est.). Manpower fit for military service: males age 16–49: 4 341 591, females age 16–49: 4 179 659 (2009 est.). Manpower reaching militarily significant age annually: male: 144 959 female: 137 333 (2009 est.).

'Illicit drugs: Tasmania is one of the world's major suppliers of licit opiate products; government maintains strict controls over areas of opium poppy cultivation and output of poppy straw concentrate; major consumer of cocaine and amphetamines.'

5

THE THINGS WE LIKE

AUSTRALIAN CULTURE—THE NATIONAL OXYMORON?

Anybody who goes to an **art gallery** is a wanker, right? There are 3.6 million wankers in Australia. Only geeks go to **libraries**, so this country has 5.4 million geeks. **Dance performances** are for poofs and fag-hags, and now we know Australia has 1.6 million people like that.

Outside of school projects, you wouldn't go sniffing dust in a **museum** unless you were a complete dag. Ring up 3.6 million as the national dag total. And anybody who has time to go wafting round a **botanic garden** needs to get a life—advice you must now offer to 5.4 million of your compatriots.

A survey released by the Bureau of Statistics under the catchy title *Attendance at Selected Cultural Venues and Events* challenges the conventional wisdom that Australia is a land of jocks and slobs. It turns out Australians are wankier, poofier, geekier and daggier than most of us imagined. Some 296 190 people are employed in 'cultural industries'.

When we go out, these are **our favourite cultural activities:**

1 **Cinema** (65 per cent of Australians go at least once a year)
2 **Sporting events** (44 per cent)
3 **Zoos and aquariums** (36 per cent)
4 **Libraries** (34 per cent)
5 **Botanic gardens** (33 per cent)
6 **Popular music concerts** (25 per cent)
7 **Art galleries** (22.7 per cent)

8   **Museums** (22.6 per cent)

9   **Theatre performances** (17.0 per cent)

10 **Musicals and operas** (16.3 per cent)

The Bureau notes that the most culturally inclined Australians are women over 45: 'Apart from popular music concerts, a higher proportion of females than males attended each venue or event. The difference was most apparent for local, state and national libraries (41 per cent of females compared with 27 per cent of males) and musicals and operas (21 per cent compared with 12 per cent).

When we stay home, here's how we use our leisure time . . .

Watching television: The average adult does it for 21 hours and 48 minutes a week. Most popular series in 2009 were *Underbelly: A Tale of Two Cities*; *Packed To The Rafters*; *NCIS*; *Masterchef*; *Talkin' 'bout Your Generation* and *Seven News*.

Listening to the radio: 14 hours and 30 minutes a week. In Sydney, the most popular broadcasters in 2009 were Alan Jones and Ray Hadley on 2GB, and Adam Spencer and Richard Glover on ABC702. Melbourne listened to Neil Mitchell on 3AW and Hamish and Andy on Fox FM.

On the internet: 9 hours and 24 minutes a week. The most popular sites were Google Search, with 12 million Australian visitors a month; Ninemsn 8.5 million; Telstra Bigpond 5.8 million; Yahoo!7 4.5 million; Fairfax Digital 4.2 million.

Reading newspapers and magazines (in print rather than online): 5 hours and 12 minutes a week.

SPORTING SPECTACLES

The ones we watch:

(In order of match-attendance and popularity on TV)

1 **AFL** (Australian Football League, aka Aussie Rules, preferred in Victoria, South Australia and Western Australia)

2 **NRL** (National Rugby League, preferred in Queensland and New South Wales)

3 **Cricket**

4 **Tennis**

5 **Horse racing**

6 **Motor sports**

7 **Rugby union**

8 **Basketball**

9 **Soccer**

10 **Netball**

The ones we do:

1 **Walking:** 18 per cent of men walk, 33 per cent of women.

2 **Aerobics/gym:** 9 per cent of men, 13 per cent of women.

3 **Swimming:** 10 per cent of men, 12 per cent of women.

4 **Golf:** 12 per cent of men, 2 per cent of women.

5 **Tennis:** 8 per cent of men, 6 per cent of women.

In the **2008 Beijing Olympics**, Australia won 14 gold medals, 15 silver and 17 bronze, placing it number 6 after China, USA, Russia, Britain and Germany.

FAVOURITE FLICKS

These are the films seen by the greatest number of Australians still alive in the 21st century, based on box office earnings adjusted for changing ticket prices:

1 **The Sound of Music** (1965) 'There is nothing more irresistible to a man than a woman who's in love with him.'

2 **Crocodile Dundee** (1986) 'That's not a knife. THAT'S a knife . . . Just kids having fun.'

3 **Titanic** (1997) 'You must do me this honour, Rose. Promise me you'll survive. That you won't give up, no matter what happens, no matter how hopeless. Promise me now, Rose, and never let go of that promise.'

4 **Star Wars** (1977) 'The Force is what gives a Jedi his power. It's an energy field created by all living things. It surrounds us and penetrates us. It binds the galaxy together.'

5 **E.T.** (1982) 'I'll be right here.'

6 **Shrek 2** (2004) 'Thank you, gentlemen. Someday I will repay you, unless of course I can't find you, or if I forget.'

7 **Lord of the Rings: The Return of the King** (2003) 'The man who can wield the power of this sword can summon to him an army more deadly than any that walks this earth. Put aside the ranger. Become who you were born to be.'

8 **Babe** (1995) 'Baa-ram-ewe, baa-ram-ewe. To your breed, your fleece, your clan be true.'

9 **Jaws** (1975) 'We're gonna need a bigger boat.'

10 **Grease** (1978) 'I just had the best summer of my life and now I have to go. It isn't fair.'

11 **The Man from Snowy River** (1982) 'There are a dozen good brood mares in that mob. I'll be back for them . . . and for whatever else is mine.'

12 **Lord of the Rings: Fellowship of the Ring** (2001) 'One ring to rule them all. One ring to find them. One ring to bring them all and in the darkness bind them.'

13 **Jurassic Park** (1993) 'God creates dinosaurs. God destroys dinosaurs. God creates man. Man destroys God. Man creates dinosaurs.'

14 **Pretty Woman** (1990) 'I appreciate this whole seduction thing you've got going on here, but let me give you a tip: I'm a sure thing.'

15 **Lord of the Rings: The Two Towers** (2002) 'Where is it? Where is it? They stole it from us, our precious. Curse them! We hates them! It's ours it is, and we wants it!'

16 **The Sting** (1974) 'Aren't you gonna stick around for your share?' 'Nah, I'd only blow it.'

17 **The Dark Knight** (2008) 'This is what happens when an unstoppable force meets an immovable object. You won't kill me out of some misplaced sense of self-righteousness. And I won't kill you because you're just too much fun. I think you and I are destined to do this forever.'

18 **Harry Potter and the Philosopher's Stone** (2001) 'You're a little scary sometimes, you know that. Brilliant. But scary.'

19 **The Lion King** (1993) 'Look inside yourself, Simba. You are more than what you have become. You must take your place in the Circle of Life.'

20 **Star Wars Episode 1: The Phantom Menace** (1999) 'There was no father. I carried him, I gave birth, I raised him. I can't explain what happened.'

21 **Forrest Gump** (1994) 'He may be the stupidest son of a bitch, but damn, he sure is fast!'

22 **The Godfather** (1972) 'My father made him an offer he couldn't refuse.'

23 **Pirates of the Caribbean: Dead Man's Chest** (2006) 'If we don't have the key, we can't open whatever we don't have that it unlocks. So what purpose would be served in finding whatever need be unlocked, which we don't have, without first having found the key that unlocks it?'

24 **The Towering Inferno** (1975) 'You know we got lucky tonight—body count's less than 200. Someday you're gonna kill ten thousand in one of these firetraps.'

25 **Finding Nemo** (2003) '. . . and the sea cucumber turns to the mollusk and says, "With fronds like these, who needs anemones?"'

AUSTRALIA'S TOP EARNERS

1 **Crocodile Dundee** (1986), box office total $48 million

2 **Australia** (2008), $37 million

3 **Babe** (1995), $37 million

4 **Happy Feet** (2006), $32 million

5 **Moulin Rouge** (2001), $28 million

6 **Crocodile Dundee II** (1988), $25 million

7 **Strictly Ballroom** (1992), $22 million

8 **The Dish** (2000), $18 million

9 **The Man from Snowy River** (1982), $17 million

10 **The Adventures of Priscilla, Queen of the Desert** (1994), $16 million

11 **Muriel's Wedding** (1994), $16 million

12 **Young Einstein** (1988), $13 million

13 **Mao's Last Dancer** (2009), $13 million

14 **Lantana** (2001), $12 million

15 **Gallipoli** (1981), $12 million

16 **The Wog Boy** (2000), $11 million

17 **The Piano** (1993), $11 million

18 **Mad Max 2** (1981), $11 million

19 **The Castle** (1997), $10 million

20 **Shine** (1996), $10 million

21 **Phar Lap** (1983), $9 million

22 **Looking For Alibrandi** (2000), $9 million

23 **Crackerjack** (2002), $9 million

24 **The Man Who Sued God** (2001), $8.5 million

25 **Ned Kelly** (2003), $8 million

26 **Kenny** (2006), $8 million

27 **Babe: Pig in the City** (1998), $8 million

28 **Crocodile Dundee in Los Angeles** (2001), $8 million

29 **Rabbit-Proof Fence** (2002), $7.5 million

30 **The Man from Snowy River II** (1988), $7.5 million

Must-see Australian films: **They're A Weird Mob** (1966); **Alvin Purple** (1973); **Picnic at Hanging Rock** (1975); **Newsfront** (1978); **My Brilliant Career** (1979); **Dead Calm** (1989); **Oscar and Lucinda** (1998); **Sirens** (1994); **Two Hands** (1999); **Ten Canoes** (2006); **Samson and Delilah** (2009).

Australian movies' share of total box office: 10 per cent in 1977; 16 per cent in 1982; 10 per cent in 1994; 8 per cent in 2000; 1.3 per cent in 2004; 4 per cent in 2008.

Source: MPDAA and AFC

TOP TELLY

The most watched programs of all time

1 **Diana Spencer's funeral** (channels 9, 7, 10, ABC), 1997

2 **Olympic opening and closing ceremonies** (7), 2000

3 **Wedding of Charles and Diana** (9, 7, 10, ABC), 1981

4 **Cathy Freeman's Olympic gold run** (7), 2000

5 **Olympic swimming events** (7), 2000

6 **The World of the Seekers** (9), 1968

7 **The Sound of Music**, first TV showing (9), 1977

8 **Roots** miniseries (10), 1977

9 **The landing on the moon** (9, 7, 10, ABC), 1969

10 **Royal Charity Concert** from the Opera House—John Farnham, Peter Allen (9), 1980

11 **Boxing: Lionel Rose v Alan Rudkin** (10), 1969

12 **LA Olympics opening ceremony** (10), 1984

13 **Tennis: Australian Open final Lleyton Hewitt v Morat Safin** (7), 2005

14 **Rugby World Cup final** (7), 2003

15 **Holocaust** miniseries (7), 1978

16 **Raiders of the Lost Ark** first TV showing (10), 1985

17 **Great Moscow Circus** (7), 1971

18 **Homicide** (7), 1971

19 **The Dismissal** miniseries (10), 1983

20 **Bodyline** miniseries (10), 1984

21 **MasterChef winner announced** (10), 2009

22 **Australian Idol final verdict** (10), 2004

23 **Commonwealth Games opening ceremony** (9), 2006

24 **The Block auction** (9), 2003

25 **September 11 reportage** on 12 September (9, 7, ABC), 2001

26 **Big Brother winner announced** (10), 2004

27 **Against The Wind** miniseries (7), 1978

28 **AFL Grand Final** (7), 2005

29 **The National IQ Test** (9), 2002

30 **World Cup Soccer Final** (9), 2002

Source: OZTAM and ACNielsen

MOST SUCCESSFUL AUSTRALIAN SERIES

1 **Homicide**, Melbourne cop drama (7), 1964–75

2 **Blue Heelers**, drama about cops in rural Victoria (7), 1994–2006

3 **The Secret Life of Us**, gritty soap (10), 2001–04

4 **The Mavis Bramston Show**, satirical sketch series (7), 1964–68

5 **SeaChange**, adult comedy soap (ABC), 1998–2000

6 **Underbelly**, fact-based crime drama (9), 2008–

7 **McLeod's Daughters**, rural soap (9), 2001–09

8 **The Comedy Company**, sketches (10), 1988–91

9 **Home and Away**, teen soap (7), 1988–

10 **The Norman Gunston Show**, comedy/chat (ABC and 7), 1975–79

11 **Neighbours**, teen soap (7 and 10), 1985–

12 **Hey Dad**, family sitcom (7), 1984–94

13 **Frontline**, media satire (ABC), 1994–97

14 **A Country Practice**, rural soap (7), 1981–93

15 **Kath and Kim**, satirical sitcom (ABC and 7), 2001–

16 **The Paul Hogan Show**, sketches (7 and 9), 1973–82

17 **Prisoner**, crime soap (10), 1979–87

18 **Number 96**, sexy soap (10), 1972–77

19 **Mother and Son**, family sitcom (ABC), 1984–94

20 **Division 4**, suburban cop drama (9), 1969–74

21 **Play School**, children's entertainment (ABC), 1966–

22 **All Saints**, hospital drama (7), 1998–2009

23 **Hey, Hey It's Saturday**, variety (9), 1971–99

24 **Border Security**, documentary about customs (7), 2004–

25 **Dancing with the Stars**, talent quest (7), 2005–

26 **Packed to the Rafters**, family dramedy (7), 2008–

27 **Sale of the Century**, game show (9), 1980–2001

28 **60 Minutes**, infotainment (9), 1979–

29 **Spicks and Specks**, musical game show (ABC) 2004–

30 **The Chaser's War on Everything**, satire (ABC), 2006–2009

Audience share of Australian networks in 2009: **Channel 7**, about 22 per cent; **Channel 9**, 20 per cent; **Channel 10**, 19 per cent; **ABC**, 15 per cent; **SBS**, 4 per cent; All **pay channels**, 20 per cent.

TOP-SELLING DVDS OF ALL TIME

1 **Finding Nemo** (2004)

2 **Lord of the Rings: Fellowship of the Ring** (2002)

3 **Harry Potter and the Chamber of Secrets** (2003)

4 **Lord of the Rings: The Two Towers** (2003)

5 **Monsters Inc.** (2002)

6 **Harry Potter and the Goblet of Fire** (2006)

7 **Harry Potter and the Prisoner of Azkaban** (2004)

8 **Lord of the Rings: Return of the King** (2004)

9 **Mamma Mia!** (2008)

10 **Pirates of the Caribbean** (2004)

11 **Shrek 2** (2004)

12 **Dirty Dancing** (2000)

13 **The Notebook** (2005)

14 **Pirates of the Caribbean 2: Dead Man's Chest** (2006)

15 **The Dark Knight** (2008)

16 **The Fast and the Furious** (2002)

17 **The Matrix** (1999)

18 **Gladiator** (2000)

19 **The Incredibles** (2005)

20 **Harry Potter and the Philosopher's Stone** (2002)

21 **Ice Age** (2002)

22 **Madagascar** (2005)

23 **Shrek** (2001)

24 **Harry Potter and the Order of the Phoenix** (2007)

25 **Cars** (2006)

26 **Star Wars Episode 2: Attack of the Clones** (2002)

27 **Australia** (2008)

28 **Casino Royale** (2007)

29 **Andre Rieu Live in Australia** (2008)

30 **Underbelly** (2008)

Source: GFK Marketing

Amount Australians spent on **buying DVDs** in 2008: $1307 million.

Amount spent on **cinema tickets** in 2008: $945 million.

TOP-SELLING ALBUMS SINCE 1986

1 **Whispering Jack**, John Farnham (1986)*

2 **Come On Over**, Shania Twain (1997)

3 **Jagged Little Pill**, Alanis Morissette (1995)

4 **Innocent Eyes**, Delta Goodrem (2003)*

5 **Music Box**, Mariah Carey (1993)

6 **Thriller**, Michael Jackson (1983)

7 **Savage Garden**, Savage Garden (1997)*

8 **Falling Into You**, Celine Dion (1996)

9 **Abba Gold**, Abba (1992)

10 **Immaculate Collection**, Madonna (1990)

11 **Recurring Dream**, Crowded House (1996)*

12 **Age of Reason**, John Farnham (1998)*

13 **The Very Best Of**, The Eagles (1994)

14 **Rumours**, Fleetwood Mac (1977)

15 **Born in the USA**, Bruce Springsteen (1984)

16 **1**, The Beatles (2000)

17 **I'm Not Dead**, Pink (2006)

18 **The Sound of White**, Missy Higgins (2005)*

19 **Don't Ask**, Tina Arena (1994)*

20 **Soul Deep**, Jimmy Barnes (1991)*

21 **Chisel**, Cold Chisel (1991)*

22 **Come Away With Me**, Norah Jones (2002)

23 **Greatest Hits Collection**, Queen (1981)

24 **Remasters**, Led Zeppelin (1990)

25 **Funhouse**, Pink (2009)

26 **Dangerous**, Michael Jackson (1991)

27 **Fever**, Kylie Minogue (2001)*

28 **Unplugged**, Eric Clapton (1992)

29 **Back To Bedlam**, James Blunt (2004)

30 **Get Born**, Jet (2003)*

*Australian made

Source: Australian Record Industry Association. CDs replaced vinyl recordings around 1985 and exact sales figures before that year are lost in the mists of time. This explains the absence of big sellers from the 1960s and 1970s, such as Elton John, The Rolling Stones, Neil Diamond, Billy Joel, Paul McCartney, Pink Floyd, The Bee Gees and Dire Straits.

ARIA HALL OF FAME

AC/DC, rock band ('Highway To Hell'), 1970s–

Peter Allen, pop singer/composer ('I Still Call Australia Home'), 1960s–92

The Angels, rock band ('Take a Long Line'), 1970s–80s

Australian Crawl, rock band ('Boys Light Up'), 1980s

Jimmy Barnes, rock singer ('Working Class Man'), 1980s–

The Bee Gees, pop group ('Spicks and Specks'), 1960s–90s

Graeme Bell, jazz bandleader and pianist ('Bull Ant Blues'), 1940s–90s

Don Burrows, jazz bandleader and flute, clarinet and sax, 1960s–80s

Brian Cadd, singer and composer ('Ginger Man'), 1960s–

Kev Carmody, singer and composer ('Cannot Buy My Soul') 1990s

Nick Cave, singer and composer ('Into My Arms'), 1970s–

Richard Clapton, pop singer ('Girls on the Avenue'), 1960s–90s

Cold Chisel, rock band ('Khe Sanh'), 1970s–80s

Daddy Cool, rock'n'roll band ('Eagle Rock'), 1970–75

Horrie Dargie, bandleader and harmonica player ('Green Door'), 1950s–99

Peter Dawson, classical and popular baritone ('Road To Gundagai'), 1900s–40s

Smoky Dawson, country singer ('The Lights of Cobb and Co'), 1940s–90s

The Dingoes, country rock band ('Way Out West'), 1970s

Divinyls, punk and rock band ('I Touch Myself'), 1981–90s

Dragon, rock band ('Are You Old Enough?'), 1970s–90s

Slim Dusty, country singer ('Pub with No Beer'), 1950s–90s

Easybeats, pop band ('Friday on my Mind'), 1960s–70s

John Farnham, pop singer ('You're the Voice'), 1960s–90s

Renee Geyer, pop/jazz singer ('Say I Love You'), 1970s–90s

Percy Grainger, classical composer and pianist ('English Country Garden'), 1920s–61

Rolf Harris, singer and comedian ('Tie Me Kangaroo Down Sport'), 1960s–

Marcia Hines, soul singer, ('Your Love Still Brings Me To My Knees'), 1970s–

Hoodoo Gurus, rock band ('What's My Scene?'), 1980s–2000s

Hunters and Collectors, rock band ('Talking to a Stranger'), 1980s–90s

Icehouse, technorock band ('Great Southern Land'), 1977–90s

Frank Ifield, country singer ('I Remember You'), 1960s–90s

INXS, rock band ('Need You Tonight'), 1980s–

Jo Jo Zep and the Falcons, rock band ('Taxi Mary'), 1970s–80s and 2000s

Col Joye, pop singer ('Be Bop A Lula'), 1950s–60s

Paul Kelly, rock/folk singer and composer ('To Her Door'), 1980s–

Jimmy Little, country singer ('Royal Telephone'), 1960s

Little Pattie (Patricia Amphlett), pop singer (He's My Blond Headed Stompie Wompie Real Gone Surfer Boy'), 1960s

Little River Band, pop band ('Reminiscing'), 1970s–90s

Lobby Loyde, guitarist ('Obsecration'), 1960s–2000s

Masters Apprentices, rock band ('Poor Boy'), 1960s–70s

Nellie Melba, opera singer ('Home Sweet Home'), 1880s–1920s

Men At Work, pop band ('Down Under'), 1970s–80s

Mental As Anything, rock band ('Live it Up'), 1970s–

Max Merritt, singer and bandleader ('Slippin' Away'), 1960s–80s

Midnight Oil, politicised rock band ('Beds Are Burning'), 1970s–90s

Russell Morris, singer ('The Real Thing'), 1960s–90s

Olivia Newton-John, pop singer ('Physical'), 1960s–90s

Johnny O'Keefe, rock singer ('Shout'), 1950s–78

Radio Birdman, rock band ('New Race'), 1970s, 1990s, 2000s

Helen Reddy, singer, ('I Am Woman'), 1970s–90s

Rose Tattoo, rock band ('Bad Boy For Love'), 1970s–80s, 2000s

Normie Rowe, pop singer ('Shakin' all Over'), 1960s

The Saints, punk band ('I'm Stranded'), 1970s–80s

The Seekers, pop group ('Georgie Girl'), 1960s–70s

Sherbet, pop band ('Howzat'), 1970s–80s

Glenn Shorrock, pop singer ('Help Is on Its Way'), 1960s–90s

Skyhooks, pop band ('Living in the Seventies'), 1970s–80s

Split Enz, pop band ('I Got You'), 1970s–80s

Joan Sutherland, opera singer ('Lucia di Lammermoor'), 1960s–80s

Billy Thorpe, rock singer ('Most People I Know Think That I'm Crazy'), 1960s–90s

Harry Vanda and George Young, pop composers ('Evie'), 1960s–90s

Ross Wilson, pop singer and composer ('Daddy Cool'), 1960s–80s

John Paul Young, ballad singer ('Love Is in the Air'), 1970s–90s

Three Australian compositions appear in the list of '500 Most Influential Rock Songs of All Time' issued by the Rock and Roll Hall of Fame in Cleveland, Ohio: 'Highway to Hell' and 'Back in Black' by **AC/DC**, and 'Beds are Burning' by **Midnight Oil**.

BEST SONGS ABOUT US

1 '**Down Under**', Men at Work (1982)

The narrator, a backpacker, finds Australia is so fashionable in Europe that a man in Brussels gave him a Vegemite sandwich. He mocks the stereotype of a land where 'women glow' and 'men chunder'.

2 '**Tie Me Kangaroo Down, Sport**', Rolf Harris (1960)

A dying stockman gives instructions to his friends, such as minding his platypus duck, Bill, and tanning his hide when he's died, Clyde. Rolf Harris now says he is ashamed of the original version, because it contained this verse: 'Let me Abos go loose, Bruce. Let me Abos go loose. They're of no further use, Bruce. Let me Abos go loose.'

3 '**Waltzing Matilda**', AB 'Banjo' Paterson (1895)

A wanderer (swagman) steals a sheep (jumbuck) and, in trying to escape the police (troopers), drowns in a pond (billabong), ultimately returning as a ghost to ask 'Who'll come a waltzing matilda with me?' A matilda is a backpack.

4 '**I Still Call Australia Home**', Peter Allen (1980)

The narrator has been to many exciting places but misses his own country. Sometimes parodied as 'I still call Australia collect', it was adopted as an advertising jingle for Qantas.

5 '**The Sounds of Then**', Gangajang (1985)

The narrator reminisces about sitting on a patio watching the lightning over the cane fields and breathing the humidity. Then he laughs and thinks, 'This is Australia'.

6 '**Shaddup You Face**', Joe Dolce (1981)

An immigrant recalls his mother's irritation when he expresses nostalgia for his homeland. She tells him Australia is not so bad, in fact 'it's a-nice-a-place'.

7 '**I am (you are, we are) Australian**', Bruce Woodley and Dobe Newton (1987)

The narrator outlines the many different backgrounds of this country's residents—Aboriginal, convict, farmer, immigrant—and concludes that we share a dream and sing with one voice.

8 '**The Pub With No Beer**', Gordon Parsons and Slim Dusty (1957)

Various outback characters—stockman, boss, swagman, blacksmith—remark that there is nothing so morbid, lonesome or drear as a bar that can only offer wine and spirits.

9 '**Click Go the Shears**', traditional (1800s)

The narrator tells how an old man beats 'the ringer' (the fastest shearer) in removing the wool from a 'bare bellied ewe', and concludes, 'He works hard, he drinks hard, and goes to hell at last'.

10 '**Up There Cazaly**', Mike Brady (1979)

The song honours Roy Cazaly, a 1930s Melbourne footballer with a talent for leaping. The crowd urges him to fly like an angel and get in there and fight.

11 '**Come On Aussie, Come On**', Mojo advertising agency (1979)

Originally written to promote Channel 9's coverage of cricket in 1979, the song names famous cricketers and boasts of the fitness of the Australian team.

12 '**Beds are Burning**', Midnight Oil (1986)

The narrator argues that it is time to give Aboriginal people their land back, or at least pay rent, because it belongs to them. Midnight Oil's 'The Power and the Passion', discussing whether Australia has too much sun and too much Uncle Sam, could be added to this list as well.

13 '**Solid Rock**', Goanna (1982)

The narrator reminds white Australians they are standing on sacred ground, controlled historically by white man, white law and white gun.

14 '**Neighbours**', Jackie Trent and Tony Hatch (1986)

The theme to the television soap suggests that with a little understanding, suburban residents can become friends.

15 '**Botany Bay**', traditional (late 1700s)

With a bizarre chorus of 'tooral-li ooral-li addity', a convicted pickpocket farewells England and anticipates seven years in Sydney. He concludes, 'Come all you young dukies and duchesses, take warning by what I do say. Mind that all is your own as you touchesses, or you'll join us in Botany Bay.'

16 '**I've Been Everywhere, Man**', Geoff Mack (1962)

The narrator boasts of his travel experiences in a list beginning with Tullamore, Seymour, Lismore and Mooloolaba. It was later parodied by Norman Gunston, who listed only Wollongong and Dapto.

17 '**True Blue**', John Williamson (1982)

The narrator wonders what it means to be Australian and whether traditional values, such as standing by a mate, would disappear if they sell us out like sponge cake.

18 '**My Island Home**', Neil Murray (1985)

The narrator, stuck in the desert (or, in the Christine Anu version, the city), recalls growing up by the sea among the salt water people.

19 '**Australiana**', Billy Birmingham, performed by Austen Tayshus (1983)

The narrator makes puns of the names of his friends at a barbecue, as in Vegie might; Nulla bores; let's go, Anna; Marie knows; my cossie, Oscar; he'll lead you astray, Leana; and where can Marsu pee, Al?

20 '**Great Southern Land**', Icehouse (1989)

The narrator describes a 'prisoner island' which was burned black by the sun and which walks alone with the ghost of time.

WHAT WE READ

The top-selling books since 1990:

1 **Harry Potter and The Philosopher's Stone**, J.K. Rowling
2 **Harry Potter and the Goblet of Fire**, J.K. Rowling
3 **Harry Potter and the Prisoner of Azkaban**, J.K. Rowling
4 **Harry Potter and the Chamber of Secrets**, J.K. Rowling
5 **The Da Vinci Code**, Dan Brown
6 **Harry Potter and the Order of the Phoenix**, J.K. Rowling
7 **Harry Potter and the Half-Blood Prince**, J.K. Rowling
8 **Harry Potter and the Deathly Hallows**, J.K. Rowling
9 **Solomon's Song**, Bryce Courtenay*
10 **The Potato Factory**, Bryce Courtenay*
11 **4 Ingredients**, Kim McCosker and Rachel Bermingham*
12 **Twilight**, Stephenie Meyer
13 **The Liver Cleansing Diet**, Sandra Cabot*
14 **Angela's Ashes**, Frank McCourt
15 **From Strength to Strength**, Sara Henderson*
16 **Four Fires**, Bryce Courtenay*
17 **The Blue Day Book**, Bradley Trevor Grieve*
18 **Men Are From Mars, Women Are From Venus**, John Gray
19 **Wild Swans**, Jung Chang
20 **Tommo and Hawk**, Bryce Courtenay*
21 **Matthew Flinders' Cat**, Bryce Courtenay*

22 **The Cook's Companion**, Stephanie Alexander*

23 **The Lord of the Rings**, J.R.R. Tolkien

24 **Your Mortgage and How to Pay it Off in Five Years**, Anita Bell*

25 **Angels and Demons**, Dan Brown

26 **Brother Fish**, Bryce Courtenay*

27 **The Footrot Flats series**, Murray Ball

28 **New Moon**, Stephenie Meyer

29 **Spotless**, Shannon Lush and Jennifer Fleming*

30 **Guinness World Records** (every year)

31 **Memoirs of a Geisha**, Arthur Golden

32 **The Persimmon Tree**, Bryce Courtenay*

33 **The Secret**, Rhonda Byrne*

34 **The Memory Keeper's Daughter**, Kim Edwards

35 **A Thousand Splendid Suns**, Khaled Hosseini

36 **Bridget Jones' Diary**, Helen Fielding

37 **The Bride Stripped Bare**, Nikki Gemmell*

38 **The CSIRO Total Wellbeing Diet**, Manny Noakes*

39 **Whitethorn**, Bryce Courtenay*

40 **Wicked**, Morris Gleitzman and Paul Jennings*

*Australian

Source: Australian Publishers Association and Nielsen BookScan

RAGS AND MAGS

These are Australia's top-selling periodicals . . .

1   **The Sunday Telegraph** (Sydney) 657 000 copies a week

2   **The Sunday Herald-Sun** (Melbourne) 617 000 a week

3   **The Sunday Mail** (Brisbane) 552 000 a week

4   **The Herald-Sun** (Melbourne) 527 000 each weekday

5   **The Herald-Sun Saturday** 515 000

6   **Women's Weekly** 491 500 a month

7   **The Sun-Herald** (Sydney) 462 000 a week

8   **Woman's Day** 408 000 a week

9   **Better Homes and Gardens** 370 000 a month

10 **The Daily Telegraph** (Sydney) 389 000 each weekday

11 **The Sydney Morning Herald Saturday** 359 000

12 **The West Australian Saturday** 343 000

13 **New Idea** 325 000 a week

14 **The Daily Telegraph Saturday** 337 000 a week

15 **Readers Digest** 325 000 a month

16 **The Sunday Times** (Perth) 321 000 a week

17 **That's Life!** 302 000 a week

18 **The Weekend Australian** 307 000 a week

19 **The Sunday Mail** (Adelaide) 306 000 a week

20 **The Age Saturday** (Melbourne) 292 000

21 **The Courier-Mail Saturday** (Queensland) 309 000 a week

22 **Super Food Ideas** 271 000 a month

23 **Take 5** 246 000 a week

24 **The Advertiser Saturday** (Adelaide) 252 000

25 **The Sunday Age** 225 000 a week

26 **TV Week** 224 000 a week

27 **The Courier-Mail** (Queensland) 220 000 a day

28 **The Age** (Melbourne) 207 000 a day

29 **The West Australian** 197 000 a day

30 **The Advertiser** (Adelaide) 188 000 a day

31 **Cosmopolitan** 166 000 a month

32 **Australian Geographic** 141 000 a month

33 **NW** 140 000 a week

34 **The Australian** 136 000 a day

35 **Who Weekly** 135 000 a week

Source: Audit Bureau of Circulations, 30/6/2009

WHAT WE SHOULD READ

'In offering this little tract to the public it is equally the writer's wish to conduce to their amusement and information.'

As opening sentences of great books go, that doesn't quite match 'It was the best of times, it was the worst of times'; 'The past is a foreign country; they do things differently there'; 'It was a bright cold day in April, and the clocks were striking thirteen'; or 'It is a truth universally acknowledged, that a single man in possession of a good fortune must be in want of a wife.'

But it's certainly more important for Australians than any of those classic teasers, because it's the beginning of the first book ever published about this country.

Sailing with the fleet that left Portsmouth in 1787 for a new Wales somewhere in the south were five men who had been commissioned by publishers to write about an adventure that was as fascinating to the British then as the moon landing was to the modern world in 1969.

The first author to get a manuscript back to his publisher in London was a marine lieutenant named Watkin Tench, and his account of the journey and the first few weeks of the settlement appeared in April 1789. *A Narrative of the Expedition To Botany Bay* was such a hit (quickly translated into French, German, Dutch and Swedish) that the publishers demanded a sequel, and *A Complete Account of the Settlement at Port Jackson* appeared in 1793. It was another bestseller. You could say Tench was Australia's first international superstar.

No doubt copies of both books were clutched in the hands of Australia's first eight free settlers when they stepped off the boat in Sydney in 1793. They were not put off by Tench's warning to potential colonists: 'If golden dreams of commerce and wealth flatter their imaginations, disappointment will follow.'

Certainly they would have enjoyed the comedy. Tench is initially puzzled when the people he calls 'the Indians' gather round a sheep pen and shout, 'Kangaroo! Kangaroo!' Later his Aboriginal friend Colbee points at a cow and asks, 'Is that a kangaroo?' When Tench identifies a two-legged furry hopper as a kangaroo, Colbee says: 'We call that a patagaran.'

It would seem the earlier explorer whom Tench calls 'Mr Cook' got the name a little wrong, at least for the language group around Sydney harbour.

If they make a movie of Tench's books, you can imagine the most memorable line from Australian cinema so far — 'That's not a knife. *That's* a knife' — being replaced by this dialogue:

Tench: 'That's not a kangaroo, that's a cow. *That's* a kangaroo.'
Colbee: 'That's not a kangaroo. That's a patagaran.'

Perhaps the women among the first free settlers were attracted by this observation in Tench's book: 'No climate hitherto known is more generally salubrious. To this cause I attribute the great number of births which happened . . . Women who certainly would never have bred in any other climate here produced as fine children as ever were born.'

Perhaps the men found comfort in this: 'To men of small property, unambitious of trade, and wishing for retirement, I think the continent of New South Wales not without inducements.'

Talk about praising with faint damns. But that's the very modest mindset from which this country grew—and from which an industry of books about our nation grew. Here's a tentative list of the most significant books about the Australian character:

1 **A Narrative of the Expedition to Botany Bay** (1789) and **A Complete Account of the Settlement at Port Jackson** (1793), now collected as **1788**, edited by Tim Flannery.

2 **The Fatal Shore**, Robert Hughes (1987)

3 **A Fortunate Life**, Albert Facey (1982)

4 **Maestro**, Peter Goldsworthy (1989)

5 **The Magic Pudding**, Norman Lindsay (1918)

6 **For the Term of His Natural Life**, Marcus Clarke (1874)

7 **Australians: Origins to Eureka**, Thomas Keneally (2009)

8 **Kangaroo**, D.H. Lawrence (1923)

9 **The Future Eaters**, Tim Flannery (1994)

10 **Cloudstreet**, Tim Winton (1991)

11 **The Macquarie Pen Anthology of Australian Literature**, edited by Nicholas Jose (2009)

12 **My Place**, Sally Morgan (1987) and **My Place**, Nadia Wheatley and Donna Rawlins (1992)

13 **Advance Australia . . . Where?**, Hugh Mackay (2008)

14 **The Secret River**, Kate Grenville (2006)

15 **The Little Book of Australia**, David Dale (2010)

POEMS

Some excerpts to get you started . . .

Bell-birds by Henry Kendall (1869)

By channels of coolness the echoes are calling,
And down the dim gorges I hear the creek falling:
It lives in the mountain where moss and the sedges
Touch with their beauty the banks and the ledges.
Through breaks of the cedar and sycamore bowers
Struggles the light that is love to the flowers;
And, softer than slumber, and sweeter than singing,
The notes of the bell-birds are running and ringing.

The Sentimental Bloke by C.J. Dennis (1915)

'Twas on a Saturdee, in Colluns Street,
An': quite by accident, o'course: we meet.
Me pal 'e trots 'er up an' does the toff:
'E allus wus a bloke fer showin' off.
'This ere's Doreen,' 'e sez. 'This 'ere's the Kid.'
I dips me lid.
'This 'ere's Doreen,' 'e sez. I sez 'Good day.'
An' bli'me, I 'ad nothin' more ter say!
I couldn't speak a word, or meet 'er eye.
Clean done me block! I never been so shy,
Not since I was a tiny little cub,
An' run the rabbit to the corner pub:
Wot time the Summer days wus dry and 'ot:
Fer me ole pot.
Gorstrooth! I seemed to lose me pow'r o' speech.
But 'er! Oh, strike me pink! She is a peach!
The sweetest in the barrer! Spare me days,
I carn't describe that cliner's winnin' ways.

The way she torks! 'Er lips! 'Er eyes! 'Er hair! . . .
Oh, gimme air!

Freedom on the Wallaby by Henry Lawson (1891)

Australia's a big country
An' Freedom's humping bluey,
An' Freedom's on the wallaby
Oh! Don't you hear 'er cooey?
She's just begun to boomerang,
She'll knock the tyrants silly,
She's goin' to light another fire
And boil another billy.
So we must fly a rebel flag,
As others did before us,
And we must sing a rebel song
And join in rebel chorus.
We'll make the tyrants feel the sting
O' those that they would throttle;
They needn't say the fault is ours
If blood should stain the wattle!

The Magic Pudding by Norman Lindsay (1918)

Politeness be sugared, politeness be hanged,
Politeness be jumbled and tumbled and banged
It's simply a matter of putting on pace,
Politeness has nothing to do with the case.
Eat away, chew away, munch and bolt and guzzle,
Never leave the table till you're full up to the muzzle.

My Country by Dorothea MacKellar (1911)

I love a sunburnt country,
A land of sweeping plains,
Of ragged mountain ranges,
Of droughts and flooding rains.

I love her far horizons,
I love her jewel-sea,
Her beauty and her terror,
This wide brown land for me.

The Man from Snowy River by Banjo Paterson (1890)

There was movement at the station, for the word had
passed around
That the colt from old Regret had got away,
And had joined the wild bush horses, he was worth a
thousand pound,
So all the cracks had gathered to the fray.
All the tried and noted riders from the stations near and far
Had mustered at the homestead overnight,
For the bushmen love hard riding where the wild bush
horses are,
And the stock-horse snuffs the battle with delight.
And one was there, a stripling on a small and weedy beast,
He was something like a racehorse undersized,
With a touch of Timor pony, three parts thoroughbred at
least,
And such as are by mountain horsemen prized.
He was hard and tough and wiry, just the sort that won't
say die
There was courage in his quick impatient tread;
And he bore the badge of gameness in his bright and fiery
eye,
And the proud and lofty carriage of his head.
And he ran them single-handed till their sides were white
with foam.
He followed like a bloodhound on their track,
Till they halted cowed and beaten, then he turned their
heads for home,

And alone and unassisted brought them back.
But his hardy mountain pony he could scarcely raise a trot,
He was blood from hip to shoulder from the spur;
But his pluck was still undaunted, and his courage fiery hot,
For never yet was mountain horse a cur.

The Overlander by unknown author (1880s)

There's a trade you all know well
And it's bringing cattle over,
On every track to the gulf and back
Men know the Queensland drover
So pass the billy round boys,
Don't let the pint pot stand there
For tonight we'll drink the health
Of every Overlander.

Nine Miles from Gundagai by unknown author (1880s)

Some blokes I know has all the luck
No matter how they fall
But there was I, Lord love a duck,
No flamin' luck at all.
I couldn't make a pot of tea
Nor keep me trousers dry
And the dog shat in the tucker-box,
Nine miles from Gundagai.
I could forgive the blinkin' tea,
I could forgive the rain;
I could forgive the dark and cold,
And go through it again.
I could forgive me rotten luck,
But hang me till I die,
I won't forgive that bloody dog,
Nine miles from Gundagai.

Clancy of the Overflow by Banjo Paterson (1889)

(The narrator, working as a clerk in the city, remembers an
old friend who has gone droving in Queensland.)

And the bush hath friends to meet him, and their kindly
voices greet him
In the murmur of the breezes and the river on its bars,
And he sees the vision splendid of the sunlit plains extended,
And at night the wond'rous glory of the everlasting stars.
I am sitting in my dingy little office, where a stingy
Ray of sunlight struggles feebly down between the houses
tall,
And the foetid air and gritty of the dusty, dirty city
Through the open window floating, spreads its foulness
over all.
And the hurrying people daunt me, and their pallid faces
haunt me
As they shoulder one another in their rush and nervous
haste,
With their eager eyes and greedy, and their stunted forms
and weedy,
For townsfolk have no time to grow, they have no time to
waste.
And I somehow rather fancy that I'd like to change with Clancy,
Like to take a turn at droving where the seasons come and go,
While he faced the round eternal of the cash-book and the
journal—
But I doubt he'd suit the office, Clancy, of The Overflow.

Said Hanrahan by John O'Brien (1921)

'We'll all be rooned,' said Hanrahan,
In accents most forlorn,
Outside the church, ere Mass began,
One frosty Sunday morn.

The crops are done; ye'll have your work
To save one bag of grain;
From here way out to Back-o'-Bourke
They're singin' out for rain.
In God's good time down came the rain;
And all the afternoon
On iron roof and window-pane
It drummed a homely tune.
And every creek a banker ran,
And dams filled overtop;
'We'll all be rooned,' said Hanrahan,
'If this rain doesn't stop.'
And stop it did, in God's good time;
And spring came in to fold
A mantle o'er the hills sublime
Of green and pink and gold.
There'll be bush-fires for sure, me man,
There will, without a doubt;
'We'll all be rooned,' said Hanrahan,
'Before the year is out.'

West by North Again by Harry 'Breaker' Morant (1895)

We'll light our camp-fires where we may, and yarn beside
their blaze;
The jingling hobble-chains shall make a music through
the days.
And while the tucker-bags are right, and we've a stick of weed,
A swagman shall be welcome to a pipe-full and a feed.

So, fill your pipe! and, ere we mount, we'll drink another nip:
Here's how that West by North again may prove a lucky trip;
Then back again: I trust you'll find your best girl's merry
face,
Or, if she jilts you, may you get a better in her place.

THE [WHOLE] NATIONAL ANTHEM

Written by Peter Dodds McCormick in 1878 and approved by referendum (against 'Waltzing Matilda' and 'God Save the Queen') in 1977, the anthem was edited down by government officials in 1984 to the two verses in **coloured type**. Here's the whole thing:

Australians all let us rejoice,
For we are young and free;
We've golden soil and wealth for toil,
Our home is girt by sea;
Our land abounds in Nature's gifts
Of beauty rich and rare;
In history's page, let every stage
Advance Australia fair!
In joyful strains then let us sing,
'Advance Australia fair!'

When gallant Cook from Albion sail'd,
To trace wide oceans o'er,
True British courage bore him on,
Till he landed on our shore.
Then here he raised Old England's flag,
The standard of the brave;
With all her faults we love her still,
'Britannia rules the wave!'
In joyful strains then let us sing
'Advance Australia fair!'

Beneath our radiant Southern Cross,
We'll toil with hearts and hands;

**To make this Commonwealth of ours
Renowned of all the lands;
For those who've come across the seas
We've boundless plains to share;
With courage let us all combine
To advance Australia fair.
In joyful strains then let us sing
'Advance Australia fair!'**

While other nations of the globe
Behold us from afar,
We'll rise to high renown and shine
Like our glorious southern star;
From England, Scotia, Erin's Isle,
Who come our lot to share,
Let all combine with heart and hand
To advance Australia fair!
In joyful strains then let us sing
'Advance Australia fair!'

Shou'd foreign foe e'er sight our coast,
Or dare a foot to land,
We'll rouse to arms like sires of yore
To guard our native strand;
Britannia then shall surely know,
Beyond wide ocean's roll,
Her sons in fair Australia's land
Still keep a British soul.
In joyful strains then let us sing
'Advance Australia fair!'

REALITY CHECK

Every time we sing 'Advance Australia Fair', we are at risk of perpetrating a fraud on the world. Do we really want to turn our schoolchildren into con artists? Have we really so many reasons to rejoice?

The annual 'Measures of Australia's Progress' report from the Bureau of Statistics suggests a certain credibility gap. Young? Free? Golden soil? Plains to share? Who are we kidding? Let's take the national boasts one by one.

'We are young' If you think half the population being older than 37 is young, you'd have to be a typical self-deluding baby boomer. The bureau reports that in the mid-1950s, 29 per cent of the population was under 15, and 8 per cent was over 65. Now only 20 per cent is under 15 and 13 per cent is over 65. The bureau stops short of suggesting we should start turning our schools into nursing homes, but remarks:

'Australia's population is ageing because of sustained low fertility—which has resulted in proportionally fewer children in the population—and increased life expectancy . . . The community faces the challenge of providing policy, programs and services to meet the changing values, behaviours and attitudes of an older population.'

'. . . and free' A much smaller proportion of us are convicts than was the case 200 years ago. The total prison population is 24 171, but that's rising as the wheels of justice grind ever more slowly: 'Over the past 10 years, the proportion of prisoners who were unsentenced (awaiting trial or sentence) increased from 12 per cent in 1994 to 20 per cent in 2004.' In 2002, one-third of cases in the higher courts were finalised in less than 13 weeks, and only 14 per cent took more than

52 weeks. In 2008, only 17 per cent took less than 13 weeks, while a quarter of cases took longer than 52 weeks.

'We've golden soil' Actually brown dust might be a better way to put it. More than a third of the driest continent on earth is effectively desert, says the bureau, and this will spread because of global warming.

'Land clearing, which is most often done for agricultural purposes, destroys plants and removes the food and habitat on which native animals rely,' says the bureau. 'Clearing allows weeds and invasive animals to spread, is a source of greenhouse gas emissions (since trees and other plants take up CO_2 from the atmosphere and carbon is released back into the atmosphere through burning or decay) and can lead to soil degradation, such as erosion and salinity, which in turn can affect water quality.'

For 2006, Australia's net greenhouse gas emissions were estimated at 576.0 megatonnes of carbon dioxide-equivalent (per capita, that's the highest rate in the world, because so much of our energy comes from coal). The bureau says: 'Australia's net emissions in 2006 were 1 per cent lower than in 2005, and 4.2 per cent above 1990 levels. The energy sector was the largest source, contributing 70 per cent of emissions, with agriculture the second largest emitter at 16 per cent.'

'Wealth for toil' We're on safer ground with wealth and toil. The bureau says there was a real growth of 21 per cent in the 'equivalised disposable income' of the average household between the mid-90s and the mid-Noughties. That's partly because we're toiling harder—average hours worked per week by a full-time employed person rose from 39.1 in 1986 to 40.1 in 2006.

Until the economic downturn, our wealth was making governments richer. The bureau says that in the year 2006, the average adult paid $14 551 in income tax, GST, stamp duty, and local council rates. That's $3400 more than in 2001.

Australians handed the federal government a total of $245 billion in 2006, up from $176 billion in 2001. About $68 billion of that was in the form of GST, and $176 billion was income tax.

'Our land is girt by sea' True enough. But we're not exactly nurturing this asset: 'The level of fishing activity has increased over the last decade to the point where almost all the major well-known fish, crustacean and mollusc resources are fully used,' says the Bureau. 'Some major species such as southern bluefin tuna, eastern gemfish and school shark have suffered serious biological depletion.'

'Our land abounds in nature's gifts' Somewhat less than before. Since 1788, seventeen of Australia's 270 species of mammals, three of the 700 species of birds, four of the 200 species of frogs and 61 of the 15 000 species of flowering plants have become extinct. Between 2000 and 2008, the number of bird and mammal species assessed as extinct, endangered or vulnerable rose from 154 to 175 (of which 69 were birds and 106 were mammals). 'Changes to the landscape and native habitat as a result of human activity has put many of these unique species at risk,' says the bureau. The creatures most in danger of extinction in 2009 included the Gilbert's potoroo, the grey nurse shark, the armoured mistfrog and the Margaret River burrowing crayfish.

'. . . renowned of all the lands' This, at least, is not just PR puff. We get 5.2 million short-term visitor arrivals a year, and they consume more than $18 billion worth of goods and services.

So perhaps we don't need to shift the anthem to 'Waltzing Matilda' for a while yet.

BEST-LOVED BRANDS

The most purchased products in Australian supermarkets and convenience stores are:

1 **Winfield** cigarettes
2 **Coca-Cola** soft drink
3 **Tip Top** bread
4 **Cadbury** chocolates
5 **Huggies** disposable nappies
6 **Nestle-Peters** ice-cream
7 **Paul's** milk
8 **Nescafé Blend 43** instant coffee
9 **Smith's Crisps** snack food
10 **Yoplait** yoghurt
11 **Kleenex Cottonelle** toilet paper
12 **Pedigree Pal** dog food
13 **McCain** frozen vegetables
14 **Whiskas** cat food
15 **Colgate** toothpaste
16 **Bega** cheese*
17 **John West** canned fish
18 **Gillette** razors
19 **Uncle Toby's** snacks
20 **Kleenex** tissues
21 **Golden Circle** fruit juice
22 **Arnott's** biscuits
23 **Weet-Bix** cereal
24 **Hans** smallgoods
25 **Old El Paso Mexican** foods
26 **Goulburn Valley** packaged fruit
27 **San Remo** pasta*
28 **Milo** milk modifier
29 **Flora** margarine
30 **Libra** tampons
31 **Leggo's** tomato products
32 **Finish** dishwashing detergent
33 **Heinz** baked beans and spaghetti
34 **Cottee's** cordials
35 **Vegemite** spread
36 **Campbell's** soup
37 **Rexona** deodorant
38 **McCain** frozen pizza
39 **Extra** chewing gum

40 **Birds Eye** frozen fish

41 **Energizer** batteries

42 **Omo** laundry detergent

43 **Pantene** shampoo

44 **Glad** plastic bags and wraps

45 **Lean Cuisine** frozen meals

46 **Mortein** insecticides

47 **Mars Bars** confectionery

48 **Snickers** confectionery

49 **Streets Golden Gaytime** ice-cream

50 **Fountain** tomato sauce

*Made by an Australian-owned company
Source: AC Nielsen

THE LITTLE BOOK OF AUSTRALIA

A DAY IN THE LIFE

The list of the most popular supermarket products on the previous page and other shopping data enable us to visualise the typical consumption pattern for a typical suburban family.

Here's a portrait of a day in the life of Michael and Julie Jones, their daughter Jessica, 19, and their son Ben, 14. If you don't recognise yourself in this, you're simply un-Australian.

The Joneses wake up and head for the bathroom, where they wipe with Kleenex Cottonelle, shampoo with Pantene and deodorise with Rexona. Michael shaves with Gillette and Julie and Jessica use Libra.

In the kitchen, Ben feeds Whiskas to Soxie and Pedigree Pal to Max, and spreads Vegemite on toasted Tip Top for himself. Michael and Julie pour Paul's into their Nescafe Blend 43 and over their Weet-Bix. Jessica swallows a glass of Golden Circle pineapple juice and a tub of Yoplait. On the way to her bus, she smokes a Winfield (the first of her four for the day) and chews an Extra so her breath won't smell. Julie puts on a load with Omo, makes Ben a sandwich with Bega cheese and Hans salami, and drives him to school in their silver Holden Commodore.

For lunch Julie heats up a can of Campbell's. Jessica has an Uncle Toby's muesli bar and a couple of squares of Cadbury's. When he gets home from school Ben has a packet of Smith's or Mars bar and a glass of Milo. When she gets home from work, Jessica has two Tim Tams and a can of Diet Coke. Julie's afternoon tea is Arnott's Shapes.

For dinner, Julie makes a sauce with Leggo's tomato paste, McCain frozen peas and John West tuna, to put over San

Remo rigatoni. Michael drinks a can of VB, Julie has a glass
of Oyster Bay sauvignon blanc. For dessert they eat Goulburn
Valley tinned fruit with Peter's ice-cream. Julie covers the
leftovers with Glad, to avoid attracting cockroaches (although
she sprays with Mortein once a week). They wash up with
Finish and brush with Colgate. Then they watch *Packed to the
Rafters*, using a remote powered by Energizer.

Jessica goes out for a drive with her boyfriend and they end up
at his place. If he used a condom, it would be Ansell, but he
doesn't, so in ten months time Jessica will be buying Huggies.

THE WAY WE EAT

'Tell me what you eat and I will tell you what you are,' said the French philosopher Anthelme Brillat-Savarin in 1826. '**A strong cup of tea and an iced Vo Vo**' said the Australian politician Kevin Rudd in 2007, suggesting how to celebrate Labor's election victory. So that's what he thinks of us?

Well, of course not. Rudd was parodying the traditional teatime of the 1950s for which the former prime minister John Howard held such nostalgia. If he'd meant to describe this nation in the Noughties, Rudd would have said 'a skim latte and two Tim Tams'.

Our **coffee consumption** (2.4 kilograms per person per year) is more than double our tea consumption. The Tim Tam (invented in 1964) outsells the Vo Vo (invented in 1906) more than ten to one. In fact, Australians eat 380 million of the insidious cuboids a year.

But that's not to say we're a nation of bikkiephiliacs. Our annual consumption rate of 7 kilos of biscuits per person falls well behind the American rate of 9 kilos per person. Nor are we a nation of chocoholics—the average Australian consumes 4.4 kilos of **chocolate** a year, while the British eat 9.2 kilos each a year and the Swiss consume 11.3 kilos each.

So if we're not chocolate biscuits, what are we? According to a survey of 1700 eaters by the economic analysts Bis Shrapnel, we're sangers and chips.

Australia's most purchased takeaway foods:

1 Sandwiches; 2 Hot chips; 3 Hamburgers; 4 Cakes/ pastries; 5 Chinese food; 6 Pizza; 7 Fried or grilled fish; 8 Ice-cream; 9 Meat pies; 10 Filled rolls.

Apparently every Australian in 2008 bought 20 sandwiches,
18 orders of potato chips and nine orders of Chinese, as part of
an expenditure of $9 billion on 1.4 billion takeaway meals—
up 3 per cent on the early Noughties.

To me, this news is more depressing than the notion we
might be the land of tea and Vo Vos. I've nothing against
the chip, but I must confess a bias against the sandwich that
began when my mother got into the habit of sending me
to school with white bread slices squashed round spaghetti
from a tin. Spaghetti sandwiches have no swapping value
and by lunchtime they're so soggy your thumb goes straight
through them. Now that I'm grown up, I will never eat a
sandwich again, not even when it's disguised as focaccia.
Informal surveys of other Australians suggest they were
equally traumatised by parents who wrapped white bread
around Peck's paste; lettuce and vegemite; Smith's crisps
and tomato sauce; peanut butter, honey and sultanas; tinned
beetroot; or mashed banana and corn flakes.

That may be why young Australians turned to other delights
on their way home. These are the portable edibles we
remember most fondly.

1   **The Chiko roll.** Inspired by the Chinese spring roll, Frank
    McEnroe of Bendigo, Victoria, created in 1951 a cylinder
    of thick dough wrapped around a mixture of chopped
    vegetables that seem to include carrot and cabbage plus
    meat which may be chicken. Deep-frozen ready to be deep-
    fried, then smeared with tomato sauce, it spread across the
    milk bars and fish and chip shops of a naive nation.

2   **The hamburger with beetroot.** The notion that any good
    burger produces pink juice which runs down your arm
    was so embedded in our national psyche that in 1999

McDonald's departed from its attempt to unite the world around the Big Mac and recruited hundreds of beetroot growers in Queensland to help develop an item unique to the Australian market: the McOz.

3 **The pizza with pineapple.** This combination horrifies people from Naples (where the pizza was invented around 100 BC) but it's a classic case of the way Australians 'adopt and adapt' to make international specialities our own.

4 **The Dagwood dog** (also known as pluto pup or battered sav). This frankfurt fried in batter was named after an American comic strip character who made fat sandwiches.

5 **The potato scallop.** Many Australians grew up unaware that a scallop could be a kind of shellfish. They thought it was a slice of potato deep fried in batter. The name probably comes from the French 'escalopes', a rounded shape.

6 **The pie floater.** A meat filled pastry boat floating in a sea of pea soup is a speciality of South Australia.

7 **Pad Thai.** Rice noodles with chilli, egg, assorted vegetables and a protein which is usually chicken but which may be duck, pork or prawn.

8 **Gozleme.** Originally from Turkey, it's a kind of pancake stuffed with spinach, cheese and/or spicy beef mince. At food markets across the land, brigades of round women with headscarves and harem pants engage in a perfectly synchronised ballet in which they roll, smear, fold, grill, turn and slice thousands of gozlemes every weekend.

9 **Butter Chicken.** Its real name is Murgh makhani, a rich concoction involving yoghurt, garlic, tomato paste, cream, chilli and multiple spices that gets children started on an addiction to Indian food.

OUR MOST INTERESTING RESTAURANTS (2010)

1 **Tetsuya's**, Sydney: Japanese/French

2 **Rockpool Bar and Grill**, Sydney: Beef and Italian

3 **Royal Mail Hotel**, Dunkeld (Victoria): French progressive

4 **The Grange**, Adelaide: Asian

5 **Star Anise**, Perth: Asian

6 **Lebrina**, Hobart: Mediterranean

7 **Buon Ricordo**, Sydney: Italian

8 **Lucio's**, Sydney: Italian

9 **Ottoman Cuisine**, Canberra: Turkish

10 **Jacques Reymond**, Melbourne: French

11 **Restaurant Two**, Brisbane: French/ Middle Eastern

12 **Stefano's**, Mildura (Victoria): Italian

13 **Universal**, Sydney: Asian progressive

14 **Aria**, Brisbane: French

15 **Sails**, Noosa (Queensland): Italian/ Asian

16 **Quay,** Sydney: French

17 **The Buffalo Club**, Brisbane: Experimental

18 **The Flower Drum**, Melbourne: Chinese

19 **Auge**, Adelaide: Italian

20 **Fellini**, Surfers Paradise: Italian

OUR MEDIA MOMENTS

In 2005 Britain's *Uncut* magazine published a list, chosen by an expert panel, of '100 mass media moments that changed the world'. Australians were as influenced as Britons and Americans by the events on the list, which was topped by Bob Dylan's 'Like a Rolling Stone' and Elvis Presley's 'Heartbreak Hotel'. It also included the films *A Clockwork Orange*, *Taxi Driver* and *The Godfather* as well as the television series *The Simpsons* and Patrick McGoohan's *The Prisoner*. The Who's song 'My Generation' and 'Purple Haze' by Jimi Hendrix were in the top 20, as was Jack Kerouac's 1950s beatnik book *On the Road*.

But Australians also had a few landmarks in their own culture—moments that went beyond mere entertainment to achieve social symbolism or historical significance. Here are 75 **media moments that stirred Australia** in the past 50 years.

1 **Graham Kennedy's** tonight shows (TV, 1957–91)

2 **Men At Work's** 'Down Under' (song, 1982)

3 **Germaine Greer's** *The Female Eunuch* (book, 1971)

4 **Barry Humphries** creates Edna Everage (recording, 1957)

5 **Peter Allen's** 'I Still Call Australia Home' (song, 1981)

6 **Number 96** shows the first bare breasts, the first gay kiss and the first terrorist bomb as a ratings booster (TV, 1972–75)

7 **Crocodile Dundee** (film, 1986)

8 **Midnight Oil's** 'Beds are Burning' (song, 1987)

9 **Homicide** tops the ratings (TV, 1966)

10 **Mad Max** (film, 1979)

11 Prime Minister Kevin Rudd's parliamentary **apology to Aboriginal people** is shown live across Australia (TV, 2008)

12 Prime Minister **Bob Hawke cries** as he confesses to being an alcoholic and an adulterer on Clive Robertson's *Newsworld* (TV, 1989)

13 **Bandstand** promotes teenage music (TV, 1958–72)

14 **Steve Irwin** holds his baby while feeding a crocodile (TV news, 2004)

15 AC/DC makes the first **rock video clip**, 'It's a Long Way to the Top' (TV, 1977)

16 After 50 years as a **top-rating network**, Channel 9 is beaten by Channel 7 (TV, 2006)

17 **Barry Jones** wins *Pick-a-Box* (TV quiz show, 1960–71)

18 **DVDs replace VHS tapes** as the preferred way of watching movies at home (2003)

19 **The Grim Reaper** commercials, warning about AIDS (advertising, from 1987)

20 Channel 9 boss Kerry Packer pulls off **Doug Mulray's Naughtiest Home Videos** halfway through the first episode (TV, 1997)

21 **Picnic at Hanging Rock** (film, 1975)

22 **Big Brother** contestant Merlin protests detention of boat people by holding up a sign 'Free the refugees' (TV, 2004)

23 The Governor-General, Sir John Kerr, is **drunk at the Melbourne Cup** (TV, 1977)

24 Singer Normie Rowe and broadcaster Ron Casey **fight over republicanism** on *The Midday Show* (TV, 1991)

25 *Oz* magazine editors beat **obscenity charges** (magazines, 1964)

26 **The Chaser** team show their arrest for breaching security at the APEC summit (TV, 2007)

27 *The Block* features **gay renovators** (TV, 2003)

28 **Yothu Yindi's** 'Treaty' (song, 1991)

29 A Catholic bishop urges viewers to sell their Ampol shares as a protest against Ampol's sponsorship of **The Mavis Bramston Show**, which has satirised organised religion (TV, 1965)

30 **Sydney Olympics** opening ceremony watched by more than 6 million (TV, 2000)

31 **Frontline** satirises *A Current Affair* (TV, 1994–97)

32 Slim Dusty's '**Pub With No Beer**' (song, 1958)

33 Graham Kennedy is **banned from live television** for doing crow imitations that start with an 'F' (TV, 1975).

34 Kerry Packer launches **World Series Cricket** (TV, 1978)

35 The first **Top 40 chart** published by Sydney Radio 2UE (music, 1958)

36 Mambo launches **loud shirts** (fashion, 1985)

37 **SBS** starts multicultural programming (TV, 1980)

38 Daddy Cool's '**Eagle Rock**' (music, 1971)

39 Austen Tayshus' **Australiana** (stage, 1983)

40 **Mother and Son** (TV, 1984–94)

41 **Triple J rock radio** goes national (music, 1995)

42 John O'Grady's book and the film of **They're A Weird Mob** celebrates immigration (book 1957, film 1966)

43 **Wogs Out of Work** makes ethnic jokes respectable (stage, 1987)

44 *Woman's Day* sells 1.4 million copies of an issue showing **paparazzi shots** of a topless Duchess of York having her toes sucked (magazine, 1992)

45 *60 Minutes* reporter **Richard Carleton** dies while reporting at the Beaconsfield mine rescue site (TV, 2006)

46 Baz Luhrmann's **Australia** becomes the second highest grossing Australian film of all time (film, 2008)

47 **Alvin Purple** sets the tone for the 70s by featuring frequent nudity (film, 1973)

48 The Easybeats' '**Friday on my Mind**' is a hit in London (song, 1966)

49 *The Aunty Jack Show* changes **from black and white to colour** mid-episode (TV, 1975)

50 Barry Humphries does **Sir Les Patterson, Minister for The Yarts** (stage, 1974–)

51 **Countdown**, and the rise of Molly Meldrum (TV, 1974–86)

52 English model Jean Shrimpton shocks Melbourne by wearing a **minidress** to the races (fashion, 1965)

53 The Moonlight State episode of **Four Corners** exposes police and political corruption in Queensland (TV, 1987)

54 Police arrest participants in the first Sydney **Mardi Gras parade** (1978) but, two decades later, become participants in the twenty-fifth Gay and Lesbian Mardi Gras (2003)

55 **Talkback radio** starts replacing Top 40 radio (1967)

56 Rolf Harris' '**Tie Me Kangaroo Down, Sport**' (song, 1960)

57 **Johnny O'Keefe** is the first successful Aussie rocker (music, TV, 1956–78)

58 **Pauline Hanson** transforms from politician to celebrity in *Dancing with the Stars* (TV, 2004)

59 **The Castle** (film, 1997)

60 **Life, Be In It** commercials, with Norm, encourage fitness (advertising, 1978–mid-1980s)

61 Mary-Anne Fahey does **Kylie Mole** on *The Comedy Company* (TV, 1988)

62 The ABC launches *Rage*, **late night music videos** (1987)

63 Charlene (Kylie Minogue) marries Scott (Jason Donovan) in **Neighbours** (TV, 1987)

64 **Kylie Minogue** introduces her buttocks in the music video of 'Spinning Around' (TV, 2000)

65 Channel 10 forced to introduce **new censorship rules** after contestant Michael exposes his penis in *Big Brother Uncut* (TV, 2005)

66 Channel 10 expels contestants Ash and John from the *Big Brother* house for '**turkey slapping**' contestant Camilla (TV, 2006)

67 Molly Jones's death in **A Country Practice** is delayed for two weeks to ensure it happens in a ratings period (TV, 1984)

68 The ABC takes **the Chaser team** off air for two weeks for a sketch which appears to satirise a charity for dying children (TV, 2009)

69 Final of *Hey Hey It's Saturday* (after 27 years) becomes the **most watched non-sporting** event of the 90s (TV, 1999)

70 *Hey Hey It's Saturday* reunions attract 3 million viewers (TV, 2009)

71 Record **Lotto draw**, with jackpot prize money of $106 million, after 10 million tickets sold (TV, 2009)

72 Australian sitcom **Hey Dad** ends after ten years (TV, 1994)

73 Final of **MasterChef** becomes the most watched non-sporting event of the Noughties (TV, 2009)

74 John Paul Young's '**Love is in the Air**' (song, 1982)

75 A masturbation plotline in family dramedy *Packed to the Rafters* provokes protests (TV, 2009)

6

OUR KIND OF PEOPLE

STIRRERS

Geoffrey Blainey

A Melbourne historian and author of a standard text about Australia, *The Tyranny of Distance*, Blainey suggested in the 1980s that multiculturalism was turning Australia into 'a cluster of tribes', that immigration from Asia should be slowed down, and that relations between Aborigines and white settlers had not been as negative as portrayed by 'the black armband view of history'.

Bob Brown

A former general practitioner elected to the Senate as a Tasmanian Greens candidate in 1996, 2001 and 2007, Brown was Australia's most consistent opposition leader between the election of John Howard and the election of Kevin Rudd, criticising Australia's detention of asylum seekers, the sending of troops to Iraq, the weakening of industrial relations laws, and the neglect of Aboriginal health. Now he concentrates on strengthening the government's policies on emissions trading and climate change.

Helen Caldicott

Adelaide-trained doctor and campaigner against nuclear weapons and nuclear power, Caldicott is president of the Washington-based Nuclear Power Research Institute.

Paul Davies

England-born professor of natural philosophy at Macquarie University in Sydney, Davies' efforts to reconcile science and faith have been translated around the globe, notably in his books *The Mind of God, God and the New Physics, The Edge of Infinity, The Cosmic Blueprint, Are We Alone?* and *How to Build a Time Machine*.

Tim Flannery
A Melbourne-born environmentalist and director of the South Australian Museum, Flannery argues, in *The Future Eaters*, that Australia needs to cut its population to below 18 million, and suggests, in *The Weather Makers*, that nuclear power would be less damaging than other energy sources.

Peter Garrett
Sydney-born Labor MP for Kingsford-Smith electorate in New South Wales and former singer with Midnight Oil, Garrett once wrote songs attacking American militarism, supported Aboriginal land rights and an Australian republic, and stood as a Senate candidate for the Nuclear Disarmament Party. He's become a lot quieter since being appointed Minister for the Environment and for the Arts.

Godwin Grech
In a case that came to be called 'Utegate', Grech, a public servant working for the Treasury in 2009, admitted faking an email which appeared to show the prime minister's office had sought favourable treatment for a man who had once lent Kevin Rudd a utility. Grech had been keen to provide the Liberal Party with ammunition against the government. The newspaper report in which he confessed contained the line: 'speaking from a psychiatric ward in Canberra'.

Germaine Greer
Melbourne-born, England-resident author and teacher, Greer launched modern feminism with *The Female Eunuch* in 1970, and continues to provoke her compatriots with books

and pronouncements on male beauty, menopause, Aboriginal reconciliation, and Australians being 'too relaxed to give a damn'.

Pauline Hanson

A Queensland-born former fish and chip shop owner, Hanson was elected as a Liberal member of federal parliament in 1996 but was disendorsed by the party and forced to sit as an independent because of speeches described as racist. She became leader of a political party called One Nation, which opposed special assistance to Aborigines and non-white immigration. Her most famous line is 'Please explain', said in response to a question about whether she was xenophobic. In 2006 she became a contestant in *Dancing with the Stars* and almost won, based on audience voting. In 2007 she launched Pauline Hanson's United Australia Party.

Taj El-Din Hilaly

Egyptian-born former Imam at the Lakemba mosque in Sydney and self-described Grand Mufti of Australia and New Zealand, Hilaly was the best known spokesperson for conservative Islam in the mid-Noughties. He was described as 'a few sandwiches short of a picnic' by Kevin Rudd after saying that Jews are trying to control the world 'through sex, then sexual perversion, then the promotion of espionage, treason, and economic hoarding', and appearing to condone rape by suggesting that women who dress provocatively are like raw meat left out for cats to eat.

Peter Jensen

Sydney-born Anglican Archbishop of Sydney, he has become the chief spokesperson for conservative evangelical Christianity. He opposes the notion that homosexuals or women are suitable people to become bishops.

Barnaby Joyce

New South Wales-born National Party Senator for
Queensland, Joyce showed a spirit of independence during
the term of the Howard government, crossing the floor
19 times to vote against his own party's positions. When Labor
came to power, he was appointed the National Party's leader
in the Senate, where he opposes action on climate change.
He became famous in 2009 for this line: 'Going to the Greens
to devise an emissions trading scheme means you are going
to have a piece of policy that comes direct from the manic
monkey cafe of inner-surburban nirvana-ville straight to you.'

Jack Mundey

Queensland-born former leader of the New South Wales
branch of the Builders Labourers Federation, Mundey argued
in the 1970s that workers had the right and duty to strike for
environmental reasons as well as for financial reasons, and
they should use 'green bans' to protect wilderness areas and
heritage buildings.

Philip Nitschke

Adelaide-born doctor and activist for the right of terminally ill
patients to end their own lives, Nitschke persuaded the Northern
Territory parliament in 1997 to legalise voluntary euthanasia, but
this was later overturned by the federal government.

Pat O'Shane

Queensland-born former Head of the NSW Department of
Aboriginal Affairs and now a magistrate working in Sydney
courts, O'Shane demonstrates a profound scepticism about
police evidence against people accused of offensive behaviour,
violent political demonstrations and property crimes.

Noel Pearson

Born in far north Queensland and trained in law at Sydney University, Pearson became an activist for Aboriginal land rights and simultaneously a critic of the 'welfare mentality' that pervades Aboriginal relations with white Australia.

John Pilger

Sydney-born, London-resident journalist and documentary maker, Pilger exposes the machinations of multinationals and the hypocrisy of governments. Some fans wish he could combine his investigative skills with Michael Moore's sense of humour, but some scandals just aren't funny.

Peter Singer

Melbourne-born professor of bioethics at the Centre for Human Values, Princeton University, and author of *Practical Ethics, Rethinking Life and Death, Animal Rights and Human Obligations* and *The President of Good and Evil*, Singer supports abortion, animal liberation and euthanasia.

Dick Smith

A Sydney-born businessman, Smith sold his retail chain, Dick Smith Electronics, in 1982 to devote himself to adventure and activism, making the first solo helicopter flight around the world and launching Dick Smith Foods in 1999 to promote Australian ownership of popular products.

GOOD SPORTS

Layne Beachley
Sydney-born surfer who describes herself as 'the most
competitive human being on the planet', Beachley won the
women's world surfing championships seven times between
1998 and 2006. She retired in 2008.

Richie Benaud
A New South Wales-born cricket all-rounder, Benaud
captained Australia from 1958 to 1964, then became a radio
and television cricket commentator. His voice was parodied in
'The Twelfth Man' comedy recordings by Billy Birmingham.

Don Bradman
Often described (particularly by the former prime minister
John Howard) as 'the greatest batsman of all time', New
South Wales-born Bradman played Test cricket between
1928 and 1948, and captained Australia in 1936 and 1937.
In 1931 the English team developed an attacking style called
'bodyline bowling' specifically to demoralise Bradman, but
his average of 99.94 runs per Test match has never been
surpassed. He died in 2001.

Greg and Trevor Chappell
Adelaide-born batsman Greg Chappell captained the
Australian cricket team between 1975 and 1977, and
again between 1979 and 1983. He is best known for 'the
underarm bowling incident' of 1981, in which he told his
younger brother Trevor to bowl the final ball of a match
along the ground, to prevent New Zealand from hitting
a six.

Kay Cottee

Sydney-born yachtswoman, Cottee was the first woman to sail solo non-stop around the world (in 1988). She celebrated rounding Cape Horn with a bottle of Grange.

Margaret Court

Our greatest female tennis player, New South Wales-born Court set the record in the 1960s for winning the most singles, doubles and mixed doubles matches—62 of them. She was ranked world number one six times between 1962 and 1970, when she won the women's singles Grand Slam. After retiring in 1977, she became a Christian fundamentalist, and said, in a speech to federal parliament in 1994: 'Homosexuality is an abomination to the Lord! Abortion is an abomination to the Lord!'

Betty Cuthbert

Our greatest runner, Sydney-born Cuthbert was nicknamed 'Golden Girl' after she won three gold medals in the 1956 Olympics and another (for the 400 metres) in 1964. Despite suffering from multiple sclerosis, she carried the torch in the Sydney Olympic stadium in 2000, where it was used by Cathy Freeman to light the flame.

Mick Doohan

Queensland-born motorcyclist, Doohan won the 500cc motorcycle world championships five times in a row between 1994 and 1998.

John Eales

Brisbane-born rugby union player (and cricketer, when young), Eales was the most successful captain in Australian rugby history, contributing to World Cup victories in 1991 and 1999. His skill as lock forward was in goal kicking, earning him the nickname 'Nobody', because 'Nobody's perfect'.

Cadel Evans
Northern Territory-born Evans is Australia's most successful mountain bike rider and road cyclist. After coming second in the Tour de France in 2007 and 2008, he became the world cycling champion in 2009 after easily winning the 262 kilometre UCI Road World Championship in Switzerland. His aggressive attitude to the media earned him the nickname 'Cuddles'.

Sarah Fitz-Gerald
Melbourne-born squash player, Fitz-Gerald won the World Open women's championships six times between 1996 and 2002.

Dawn Fraser
Sydney-born swimmer, Fraser was the first woman to swim 100 metres in less than a minute and won four gold medals at the Olympics of 1956, 1960 and 1964, but was banned from the 1968 Olympics for disobedient behaviour. She served in NSW parliament as the Independent MP for Balmain from 1988 to 1991.

Cathy Freeman
Queensland-born sprinter, Freeman was named Australian of the Year in 1998. She won the gold medal in the 400 metres race at the 2000 Olympics, and carried both the Australian flag and the Aboriginal flag for her victory lap. She retired in 2004.

Ryan Girdler
Sydney-born rugby league player, Girdler played centre for the Penrith Panthers between 1993 and 2004. During the 2000

State of Origin he scored a record 32 points in one game, and he was the first player to score 100 tries and kick 500 goals in a career.

Andrew and Matthew Johns

Australia's greatest rugby league halfback, New South Wales-born Andrew 'Joey' Johns earned 2176 points in his first-grade career (1994–2007)—higher than any player in premiership history. In the late Noughties he admitted using ecstasy as treatment for depression, but this scandal was overshadowed by his brother Matthew's admission of involvement in a group sex act during a football tour of New Zealand in 2002. In 2009 'Matty' lost his job as a football commentator for Channel 9.

Rod Laver

Our greatest tennis player, Queensland-born Laver was ranked world number one for seven years (1964–70). He won Wimbledon four times and the men's singles Grand Slam (Wimbledon, French Open, US Open and Australia's Davis Cup) in 1962 and again in 1969.

Walter Lindrum

Best known nowadays because his gravestone in Melbourne General Cemetery is shaped like a billiard table (with balls and cue), Kalgoorlie-born Lindrum set world records for playing billiards in the 1930s that have never been broken—for example, 1900 consecutive scoring shots in 175 minutes, totalling 4137.

Tony Lockett

Victoria-born AFL player, 'Plugger' Lockett scored the most goals in a career (1360 between 1983 and 2002), playing for St Kilda and the Sydney Swans.

Michael Milton

The world's greatest one-legged skier, Canberra-born Milton won four gold medals at the 2002 Winter Paralympics and holds the record as the fastest skier on one leg (213.65 kilometres per hour in 2006).

Greg Norman

Queensland-born golfer, 'The Great White Shark' won the British Open in 1986 and 1993 and spent 331 weeks ranked as the world's number one player between 1976 and 1995. In 2008 he married the former US tennis champion Chris Evert, and in 2009 separated from her.

Stephanie Rice

Brisbane-born swimmer, she won three gold medals at the Beijing Olympics in 2008, and holds the world record for the 400 metres individual medley.

Lionel Rose

Victoria-born boxer, Rose became Bantamweight Champion of the World in 1968 (when he was named Australian of the Year). He is the first (and only) Aboriginal man to win a world title.

Anne Sargeant

Sydney-born netball shooter, Sargeant played in Australia's world-beating teams in 1979 and 1983 and captained Australia from 1983 to 1987.

Louise Sauvage

Perth-born wheelchair racer Sauvage, whose motto is 'You never know what you can achieve until you try', won gold medals at three Olympic games and the Boston Marathon four times.

Ian Thorpe

Our greatest ever swimmer, Sydney-born Thorpe won five Olympic gold medals—more than any other Australian. He retired in 2006, holding world records in 200-, 400- and 800-metre freestyle. Nicknamed 'Thorpedo', he became a role model for metrosexuality.

Shane Warne

The greatest leg spin bowler of all time, Melbourne-born Warne took 620 wickets in 125 Tests between 1991 and 2005, undistracted by media exposure for his womanising, and charges of bringing the game of cricket 'into disrepute'.

Steve Waugh

Australia's most successful cricket captain, Sydney-born Waugh played in 164 Tests between 1984 and 2004, and captained the team for five years. In 1996 he was ranked as the world's leading Test batsman. In retirement he set up the Steve Waugh Foundation, for children with rare illnesses, and wrote an autobiography, *Out of My Comfort Zone*. His nicknames were 'Tugga' and 'Iceman'. His twin brother Mark was a successful batsman, bowler and slip fielder.

Karrie Webb

Queensland-born Webb is Australia's most successful female golfer. She won the US Women's Open in 2000 and 2001 and the British Women's Open in 1999 and 2002.

Mark Webber

New South Wales-born Formula One racing car driver (and tennis player), Webber won the German Grand Prix in 2009—the first Australian to win a Grand Prix since Alan Jones in 1981. It was his 130th race. Earlier that year, he had come second in the Chinese, British and Turkish Grands Prix.

INVESTIGATORS

Elizabeth Blackburn
Hobart-born Professor of Biology at the University of
California, San Francisco, Blackburn won a Nobel Prize for
Medicine in 2009 for her discovery of telomeres, caps on the
ends of chromosomes which protect genetic information. Her
research relates to the effects of ageing and cancer.

Graeme Clark
Sydney-born Professor of Otolaryngology at the University
of Melbourne, Clark's invention of the bionic ear, or
'multi-channel cochlear implant', has helped 60 000 deaf adults
to hear. He is now investigating the feasibility of a 'bionic eye'.

Derek Denton
Launceston-born founder of the Howard Florey Institute of
Experimental Physiology and Medicine at the University of
Melbourne, Denton discovered the link between salt and high
blood pressure.

Peter Doherty
Brisbane-born Professor of Microbiology and Immunology
at Melbourne University and Professor of Pediatrics at the
University of Tennessee, Doherty won a Nobel Prize for
Medicine in 1996 for 'discoveries concerning the specificity
of the cell-mediated immune defence'.

(Australia's **other Nobel-Prize winning scientists** have been
William Lawrence Bragg and his father, William Henry
Bragg, for X-ray crystallography in 1915; Howard Florey for
work on antibiotics in 1945; Frank Macfarlane Burnet for
immunology in 1960; John Eccles for study of the nervous

system in 1963; John Cornforth for study of enzyme catalysed reactions in 1973; and Barry Marshall and Robin Warren in 2005 for discovering the role of bacteria in ulcers.)

Ian Frazer

Edinburgh-born Dr Frazer now heads the University of Queensland Centre for Immunology and Cancer Research at the Princess Alexandra Hospital, Brisbane. He was named Australian of the Year in 2006 for developing a vaccine which prevents the disease associated with the papilloma virus that causes most cervical cancers.

Basil Hetzel

London-born Professor of Medicine at the Queen Elizabeth Hospital, University of Adelaide, Foundation Professor of Social and Preventive Medicine at Monash University, and the First Chief of the CSIRO Division of Human Nutrition, Hetzel's work helped eradicate iodine deficiency in many countries.

Silviu Itescu

Melbourne-trained director of transplantation immunology at Columbia University Medical Centre in New York, Itescu showed that adult stem cells from bone marrow could be used to repair damaged hearts.

Barry Marshall

Kalgoorlie-born gastroenterologist at the University of Western Australia, Marshall defeated sceptics by swallowing a culture of the bacteria *Helicobacter pylori*, giving himself gastritis, then curing it with antibiotics, while investigating the cause of stomach ulcers with pathologist Robin Warren in the mid-1980s. This transformed the way most ulcers are tested and treated. In 2005, Marshall and Warren won the Nobel prize for medicine.

Robert May

Sydney-born president of the Royal Society in London,
May studied theoretical physics at Sydney University and
mathematical biology at Oxford then became chief scientific
adviser to the British government. He specialises in the
dynamics of populations, communities and ecosystems, looking
at the impact of AIDS, biodiversity and global warming.

William McBride

The allegations that Sydney-born gynaecologist McBride
took ethical shortcuts in his later research do not diminish
his discovery in the 1960s that the morning sickness drug
thalidomide caused deformities in babies.

Donald Metcalf

New South Wales-born Professor Emeritus at the Walter
and Eliza Hall Institute of Medical Research in Melbourne,
Metcalf discovered 'colony stimulating factors' in blood cell
formation, which revolutionised the treatment of cancer and
earned him the title 'the father of hematopoietic cytokines'.

Gustav Nossal

Austrian-born adviser to the World Health Organization on
eradicating childhood diseases, Nossal, after thirty years of
directing medical research at Melbourne's Walter and Eliza
Hall Institute, now chairs the $A1.4 billion Bill and Melinda
Gates Program for immunising children in poor nations.

Kennedy Shortridge

Queensland-born Emeritus Professor of Microbiology at the
University of Hong Kong, Shortridge's research on the spread
of respiratory viruses from poultry to humans is credited with
averting an influenza pandemic in 1997.

Allan Snyder

United States-born Professor of Science and the Mind at
Sydney University, Snyder's research on how light travels
along optical fibres is central to modern telecommunications
technology. He also founded the Centre for the Mind at the
Australian National University to investigate the talents of
autistic savants and the potential of the brain.

Fiona Stanley

Sydney-born chief executive of Perth's Australian Research
Alliance for Children and Youth, Stanley's investigations into
the causes and prevention of birth defects and neurological
disorders led her to become a lobbyist on behalf of
underprivileged children.

Fiona Wood

Born in Britain, Wood completed her medical training in
Perth and became Director of Royal Perth Hospital's Burns
Unit and Professor with the School of Paediatrics and Child
Health at the University of Western Australia. She has
patented her invention of spray-on skin for burns victims.
She was named Australian of the Year in 2005 for her work
repairing the skin of victims of the Bali bombings, and was
rated the most trusted person in Australia in a 2009 *Reader's
Digest* poll.

COMMUNICATORS

Col Allan
New South Wales-born former editor of Rupert Murdoch's
Sydney tabloid the *Daily Telegraph*, Allan became the editor
in 2003 of Murdoch's main American tabloid *The New York
Post*, and earns $US600 000 a year.

Peter Carey
Melbourne-born novelist and former head of a Sydney
advertising agency, Carey has won the Miles Franklin Award
three times for the novels *Bliss, Oscar and Lucinda* and *Jack
Maggs*, and Britain's Booker Prize for *Oscar and Lucinda* and
The True History of the Kelly Gang.

J.M. Coetzee
South African-born and Adelaide-resident novelist, John
Maxwell Coetzee won the Booker Prize in 1983 for *Life and
Times of Michael K* and again in 1999 for *Disgrace*, and then
won the Nobel Prize for Literature in 2003 as an author 'who
in innumerable guises portrays the surprising involvement of
the outsider'.

Bryce Courtenay
South African-born ex-advertising executive, Courtenay is
our most successful author, totalling five million sales for
his novels, including *The Power of One, The Potato Factory,
Tommo and Hawk, Jessica* and *Solomon's Song*.

Annabel Crabb
Adelaide-born political satirist, Crabb made her name in the
late Noughties through an acerbic column in the *Sydney*

Morning Herald and went on to provide political commentary for the ABC on radio, television and website.

Helen Garner
Melbourne-born writer Garner has moved from novels such as *Monkey Grip* to social analyses such as *The First Stone* (about sexual harassment) and *Joe Cinque's Consolation* (about drug addiction and murder).

John B. Fairfax
The heir of the Fairfax dynasty, which started the *Sydney Morning Herald* in 1841, he owns Rural Press, publisher of many country newspapers, and is a large shareholder in Fairfax Media, publisher of the *Sydney Morning Herald* and *The Age*. His personal fortune is estimated by *BRW* magazine as $618 million.

Robert Hughes
Sydney-born art critic for *Time* magazine, Hughes became one of America's most influential social commentators through such books as *Culture of Complaint, American Visions, Nothing if Not Critical* and *The Shock of the New*. His *The Fatal Shore* is an essential history of early Australia.

Clive James
Sydney-born writer, poet, critic and comedian, James is one of Britain's most influential media commentators, best known here for his hilarious autobiography *Unreliable Memoirs*.

Thomas Keneally
Sydney-born novelist, historian and activist for a republic, Keneally won Britain's Booker Prize for *Schindler's Ark* (adapted by Steven Spielberg as the film *Schindler's List*) and analysed Australia's hang-ups with *Bring Larks and Heroes, The Chant of Jimmy Blacksmith* and *The Cut Rate Kingdom*.

Jill Ker Conway

New South Wales-born writer Conway wrote an auto-
biographical series starting with *The Road from Coorain*,
ran Smith College, America's largest university for women,
and was chairman of Lend Lease for two difficult years.

Rupert Murdoch

Melbourne-born chief executive of US-based News
Corporation, Murdoch controls 70 per cent of Australia's
newspapers and owns media on most continents through such
outlets as Fox, Sky, *The Times* and *The Australian*. He failed to
dissuade his son Lachlan from leaving his job with News Corp
in New York and returning to Sydney. Now Murdoch's heir-
apparent seems to be his younger son James.

Les Murray

Country New South Wales-born poet, Murray's collections
include *The Vernacular Republic, Lunch and Counter Lunch*
and *Subhuman Redneck Poems*, which won the T.S. Eliot
literary prize in 1996.

David Nunan

Broken Hill-born professor of applied linguistics at the
University of Hong Kong, Nunan's teachings have spread
the English language throughout Asia. Students in Japan,
South Korea and China buy more than a million copies of his
textbooks every year.

Wilga Rivers

A Melbourne-born linguist and professor emerita of romance
languages and literature at Harvard University, Rivers has been
awarded the Legion d'Honneur by the French government.

Dorothy Rowe

Newcastle-born psychologist Rowe was voted one of the six wisest people in Britain in the 1990s for her books and TV appearances on conquering fear and depression.

Kerry Stokes

With the death of Kerry Packer and the decision of James Packer to sell off many of his media assets, Perth-born Stokes became the most powerful communications mogul resident in Australia (since Rupert Murdoch lives in America). He owns the highest rating television network (Channel 7), a $500 million chunk of Telstra, a controlling interest in *The West Australian* newspaper and Pacific Publications, which produces a third of Australia's top-selling magazines. His personal fortune is estimated at $1.9 billion.

Robert Thomson

Victoria-born journalist Thomson trained at the *Sydney Morning Herald* and became editor of *The Times* of London in 2004, and editor-in-chief of Dow Jones and publisher of Rupert Murdoch's *Wall Street Journal* in 2008.

David Williamson

A Melbourne-born engineer by training, Williamson is our most successful playwright and screenwriter, with hits such as *The Removalists*, *Don's Party*, *The Club*, *Gallipoli*, *Emerald City* and *Phar Lap*.

Tim Winton

Perth-born novelist and surfing enthusiast Winton won the Miles Franklin Award for *The Shallows* in 1984, *Cloudstreet* in 1992, *Dirt Music* in 2002 and *Breath* in 2009.

HELPERS

David Bussau
New Zealand-born, Sydney-based founder of Opportunity International, Bussau tackles poverty by arranging loans to small businesses in developing countries.

Simon Chesterman
Melbourne-born executive director of the Institute for International Law and Justice at New York University, Chesterman is the author of *Just War or Just Peace? Humanitarian Intervention and International Law*. He advises the UN on helping countries make the transition from dictatorship to democracy.

Margaret Cossey
New South Wales-born teacher of literacy to urban and rural Aboriginal children, Cossey created, edited and published a series called Indij Readers, in which Aboriginal writers and artists told stories that related to the children's culture.

Mick Dodson
West Australia-born Dodson was the first Aboriginal person to graduate in law in Australia (from Monash University) and is now Director of the Australian National University's National Centre for Indigenous Studies. He was named Australian of the Year in 2009 for his work towards reconciliation.

John Fawcett
Perth-born Bali-based international projects director for the John Fawcett Foundation, Fawcett's clinics treat thousands of Indonesian children with diseases of the eyes, palate and chest.

Catherine Hamlin
Sydney-born director of Addis Ababa Fistula Hospital in
Ethiopia, Hamlin has worked since the 1960s on performing
and teaching surgery for women injured while giving birth.

Fred Hollows
A New Zealand-born opthalmologist who spent 30 years trying
to prevent blindness caused by trachoma among Aboriginal
people. He died in 1993, but his foundation continues to
build clinics and lens factories throughout Africa and Asia.

Lee Kernaghan
Victoria-born country singer Kernaghan was named Australian
of the Year in 2008 for his fundraising work for farmers
suffering through drought.

Ian Kiernan
Sydney-born businessman, yachtsman and environmentalist
Kiernan was alarmed by the extent of ocean pollution in
the 1990s and organised the Clean Up Australia movement,
which has now grown into the Clean Up The World
movement with 40 million volunteers in 120 countries.

Mahboba Rawi
Kabul-born, Sydney-based founder of the aid agency
Mahboba's Promise, Rawi escaped Afghanistan as a refugee
and now returns to build orphanages, schools and hospitals for
women and children.

ENTERTAINERS

Gillian Armstrong

Melbourne-born director Armstrong won an Australian Film Institute (AFI) award for her film *My Brilliant Career* but is best known in America for *Little Women*, *Charlotte Gray* and *Death Defying Acts*.

Eric Bana

Melbourne-born former standup comedian Bana featured in *The Castle* and *Chopper* here before featuring in Hollywood blockbusters *Troy*, *Munich*, *Hulk*, *Black Hawk Down*, *Star Trek* and *The Time Traveller's Wife*. He returned to Australia in 2007 to make *Romulus My Father*.

Bruce Beresford

Sydney-born director Beresford won AFI awards for his films *The Fringe Dwellers*, *Breaker Morant* and *Don's Party*, and was Oscar-nominated for *Tender Mercies*. He is best known for *Driving Miss Daisy* and *Mao's Last Dancer*.

Hamish Blake

Melbourne-born comedian Blake has become the favourite guest on TV talk shows and game shows because of his capacity to be smart, silly, witty and weird. His drive-time radio show with Andy Lee on the Today network rates in every capital.

Cate Blanchett

Melbourne-born actress Blanchett won an Oscar for her role in *The Aviator*, a BAFTA and a Golden Globe for *Elizabeth*, an AFI for *Thank God He Met Lizzie*, and is much admired for her Galadriel in *The Lord of the Rings* trilogy.

Bryan Brown

Sydney-born actor/producer Brown won AFI awards for his roles in *Breaker Morant* and *Two Hands* and perfected the blunt but decent Aussie persona in *Cocktail*, *Gorillas in the Mist*, *Tai Pan* and *A Town Like Alice*.

Jane Campion

New Zealand-born and Sydney-trained director Campion won an AFI for her film *Sweetie* and an Oscar for *The Piano*. She also made *Portrait of a Lady*, *In the Cut* and *Angel at My Table*.

Nick Cave

Melbourne-born, London-based singer and composer Cave, a former heroin addict, is better known for albums than singles, and his tortured punk ballads include 'From Her to Eternity', 'Tupelo', 'Sad Waters', 'Into My Arms' and 'The Weeping Song'. In 2005 he wrote an Australian 'Western' movie, *The Proposition*.

Toni Collette

Sydney-born actress Collete was Oscar-nominated for her role in *The Sixth Sense*, and won AFI awards for *Muriel's Wedding*, *Lillian's Story*, *The Boys* and *Japanese Story*. In 2006, she attempted a singing career, and in 2009 she won an Emmy award for her TV series, *United States of Tara*.

Russell Crowe

New Zealand-born, Sydney-trained actor Crowe is best known for his bad temper and winning an Oscar for *Gladiator*, a BAFTA for *A Beautiful Mind*, and AFIs for *Romper Stomper* and *Proof*.

Judy Davis
Perth-born actress Davis was Oscar-nominated for *Husbands and Wives* and *A Passage to India*, and won a BAFTA for *My Brilliant Career*, AFIs for *Winter of Our Dreams*, *High Tide* and *Children of the Revolution*, and an Emmy for *Life With Judy Garland*.

John Farnham
English-born pop singer Farnham had his first hit with 'Sadie The Cleaning Lady' in 1967, and in the 80s released Australia's top-selling album, *Whispering Jack*, and single, 'You're the Voice'. In 2009, he became famous for the frequency of his final concerts. The phrase 'more farewells than Melba' was replaced by 'More farewells than Farnham'.

Mel Gibson
New York-born, Sydney-trained actor/director/producer Gibson is best known here for the *Mad Max* trilogy and internationally for making (with his Icon Films partner Bruce Davey) *The Passion of the Christ*. He won AFIs for *Tim* and *Gallipoli*, and an Oscar for directing *Braveheart*, and court-ordered alcoholism treatment for making anti-Semitic remarks to a traffic cop in 2006.

Delta Goodrem
Sydney-born singer, pianist and composer Goodrem had hits with the singles 'Born to Try' and 'Lost Without You' and her album *Innocent Eyes* after starring in *Neighbours*.

Rachel Griffiths
Melbourne-born actress Griffiths was Oscar-nominated for her role as Hilary in *Hilary and Jackie*, and won an AFI for *Muriel's Wedding* and a Golden Globe for the TV series *Six Feet Under*. She stars in the series *Brothers and Sisters*.

Reg Grundy

Sydney-born television game show host and producer Grundy created *Sale of the Century*, *The Restless Years*, *Prisoner* and *Neighbours* here, then built an international empire of more than 200 dramas and game shows.

Rolf Harris

Perth-born singer, painter and comedian, Harris' wobble board carried Australia's image to London, to the tune of 'Tie Me Kangaroo Down, Sport', long before Kylie's buttocks and Elle's breasts.

Jennifer Hawkins

Newcastle-born model who won the Miss Universe contest in 2004, Hawkins created a television career by appearing in *The Great Outdoors*, *Dancing with the Stars* and Myer commercials.

Paul Hogan

Lightning Ridge-born actor Hogan made his name in the 1970s with TV sketch comedy and then created our most successful international movie, *Crocodile Dundee*. He also 'put another shrimp on the barbie' in tourism commercials. In 2009 he was investigated by the Tax Office.

P.J. Hogan

Brisbane-born writer director 'the other Paul Hogan' made *Muriel's Wedding* here, then went to Hollywood and made *My Best Friend's Wedding*, *Peter Pan*, and *Confessions of a Shopaholic*.

Barry Humphries

Melbourne-born comedian Humphries has made Dame Edna Everage the toast of London and New York stage and

television, while his politician Sir Les Patterson keeps coming
home to haunt us.

Natalie Imbruglia
Sydney-born singer and composer Imbruglia starred in
Neighbours before moving to London and recording the
number-one single 'Torn'. She was married to the singer-
composer Daniel Johns.

Steve Irwin
Melbourne-born presenter of the TV documentary series *The
Crocodile Hunter*, Irwin became world notorious in 2004 for
feeding a crocodile while holding his baby son. He was killed
by a stingray in 2006.

Hugh Jackman
Sydney-born and Perth-trained actor/singer Jackman won
a Tony award for his Broadway portrayal of Peter Allen in
The Boy from Oz, and then played amnesic lycanthropes in
Van Helsing and the *X-Men* series of films. In 2008 People
magazine named him sexiest man alive and he starred in
Australia, and in 2009 he hosted the Oscars.

Nicole Kidman
Hawaii-born, Sydney-trained actress Kidman is our highest
paid performer, winning an Oscar for *The Hours*, a Golden
Globe for *Moulin Rouge*, and an AFI for the TV miniseries
Vietnam. In Australia, her most successful film was *Australia*.

Anthony LaPaglia
Adelaide-born actor LaPaglia is best known for playing New
York cops and criminals. He won an AFI for *Lantana*, and a
Golden Globe for the TV series *Without a Trace*.

Heath Ledger

Perth-born actor Ledger started in *Home and Away* and went on to play strong silent types in *Brokeback Mountain*, *Ned Kelly*, *The Patriot*, *Two Hands*, *A Knight's Tale* and *10 Things I Hate About You*. He died in 2008 and won a posthumous Oscar for his role as The Joker in *The Dark Knight*.

Baz Luhrmann

New South Wales-born director Luhrmann was Oscar-nominated for his film *Moulin Rouge*, and won an AFI for *Strictly Ballroom*, and a BAFTA for *Romeo+Juliet*. In 2009 his *Australia* became the second-highest grossing Australian film in history.

Robert Luketic

Sydney-born writer-director Luketic made a comedy short called *Titsiana Booberini* in Australia, then moved to Hollywood to make *Legally Blonde*, *21*, *Monster-in-Law* and *The Ugly Truth*.

Charles Mackerras

United States-born, Sydney-trained oboist and conductor Mackerras has been chief conductor of opera companies throughout Europe and conducted the first concert for the opening of the Sydney Opera House in 1973.

Elle Macpherson

Sydney-born model, actress and entrepreneuse Macpherson was nicknamed 'The Body' after she became our first international supermodel. She also acted in *Sirens*, *The Edge*, *Batman and Robin*, and the TV series *Friends*.

Ray Martin

Sydney-born former presenter of A *Current Affair* and *Midday Show*, Martin was once regarded as the most credible journalist/interviewer on commercial television. He has won several Logie awards and now narrates occasional features for Channel 9 programs such as *60 Minutes*.

Eddie McGuire

Melbourne-born former AFL commentator, he became host of *Who Wants To Be A Millionaire* in 1999 and in 2006 became CEO of the Nine network. By 2009 he was back hosting an afternoon game show called *Hot Seat*.

Ian 'Molly' Meldrum

As host of the ABC pop music show *Countdown* between 1974 and 1987, country Victoria-born Meldrum pioneered an inarticulate interviewing style that amazed and amused the nation. He perfects this style with variety show appearances, wearing a cowboy hat.

Shaun Micallef

Adelaide-born lawyer, writer, actor and comedian, Micallef is the only other contender for John Clarke's title of 'Court Jester of Australia'. His TV triumphs have varied from cult satires (*Micallef Tonight, Newstopia*) to mass market game shows (*Thank God You're Here, Talkin' Bout Your Generation*).

George Miller

Queensland-born director Miller won AFIs for *Flirting*, *The Year My Voice Broke* and *Mad Max 2* and was Oscar-nominated for *Babe* and *Lorenzo's Oil*. He directed *Happy Feet*, which won the Oscar for best animated feature in 2007.

A different (Scottish-born) George Miller directed *The Man from Snowy River* and the TV series *ANZACs* and *All the Rivers Run*.

Kylie Minogue
Melbourne-born singer and dancer Minogue first starred in *Neighbours* and then had a hit in 1988 with 'Locomotion'. She moved to London and made sexy music videos to promote 'Spinning Around' and 'Can't Get You Out of My Head', which attracted a gay male following. She returned to performing in 2006 after treatment for breast cancer.

Simon Morley, Justin Morley and David Friend
Melbourne-born comedians Morley, Morley and Friend exported their 'genital origami' show *Puppetry of the Penis* to the world.

Sam Neill
Ireland-born, New Zealand-raised actor Neill is claimed by us because he won an AFI for *A Cry in the Dark* and played Australians in *My Brilliant Career, Mary Bryant, Jessica, The Dish, Sirens* and *Dead Calm*, and talked American almost as fluently as Australian actors in the two *Jurassic Park* films.

Bert Newton
Originally the straight man to Graham Kennedy, Melbourne-born Newton has used his wit, his roundness and his orange hairpiece to charm audiences via the Logie Awards, TV commercials, the daily shopping show *Good Morning Australia*; the game show *Bert's Family Feud* and the nostalgia show *20 to 1*.

Phillip Noyce
Griffith-born director Noyce won AFIs for *Newsfront*
and *Rabbit-Proof Fence* but is best known for the thrillers
Dead Calm, Patriot Games, Clear and Present Danger
and *Sliver.*

Frances O'Connor
England-born and Perth-raised actress O'Connor is best
known here for *Kiss or Kill,* in Britain for *Madame Bovary* and
Mansfield Park and in the US for *Bedazzled* and *AI: Artificial
Intelligence* and the TV series *Cashmere Mafia.*

Miranda Otto
Brisbane-born actress Otto played Lindy Chamberlain in the
TV miniseries *Through My Eyes,* and is best known in the US
for the *Lord of the Rings* trilogy, *War of the Worlds* and the TV
series *Cashmere Mafia.*

Guy Pearce
England-born and Geelong-raised actor Pearce began his career
as a muscleman in *Neighbours* and is now famously skinny. He
starred in *The Adventures of Priscilla, Queen of the Desert, LA
Confidential, Memento, The Time Machine* and *Two Brothers.*

Richard Roxburgh
Albury-born actor Roxburgh won an AFI for *Doing Time
For Patsy Cline* and then got typecast as a villain in *Moulin
Rouge, Mission Impossible 2, Van Helsing* and *The League of
Extraordinary Gentlemen.*

Geoffrey Rush
Toowoomba-born actor Rush won an Oscar for *Shine,* a
BAFTA for *Elizabeth,* an Emmy for *The Life and Death of*

Peter Sellers, and acclaim from children for *Pirates of the Caribbean*. In 2009, he won a Tony award for his Broadway performance in *Exit the King*.

Fred Schepisi
Melbourne-born director Schepisi won AFIs for *A Cry in the Dark* and *The Devil's Playground*, and is best known for *Roxanne*, *The Russia House* and *Last Orders*.

John Seale
Queensland-born cinematographer Seale won an AFI for *Careful, He Might Hear You* and an Oscar for *The English Patient*, and was Oscar-nominated for *Witness*, *Rain Man* and *Cold Mountain*.

Dean Semler
South Australia-born cinematographer Semler won an Oscar for *Dances with Wolves* and AFIs for *Dead Calm* and *My First Wife*, and is best known for *City Slickers*, *Bruce Almighty* and *The Longest Yard*.

Magda Szubanski
Best known as the unfortunate Sharon in *Kath and Kim*, the British-born comedian was rated Australia's most liked person for most of the Noughties. She also played the farmer's wife in *Babe* and was the voice of Miss Viola in *Happy Feet*.

Jack Thompson
Sydney-born, Queensland-educated staple of 70s Australian movies such as *The Man From Snowy River*, *Breaker Morant* and *Sunday Too Far Away*, Thompson found success playing heavies in Hollywood films such as *Star Wars II: Attack of the Clones*, *Midnight in the Garden of Good and Evil* and

Leatherheads. In 2008 he started hosting the TV series *Find My Family.*

Barry Tuckwell
Melbourne-born classical trumpeter Tuckwell was the most recorded horn player in the world, with 45 albums and three Grammy nominations, before he retired in the 1990s.

Naomi Watts
England-born, Sydney-raised actress, Watts started in the soap *Home and Away* in 1991 and got noticed by Hollywood in 2001 after her role in *Mulholland Drive.* She was nominated for an Oscar and a BAFTA for *21 Grams*, and starred in *The Ring* and *King Kong.*

Hugo Weaving
Nigeria-born, Sydney-trained actor Weaving won AFIs for *Proof* and *The Interview*, found fame in *The Adventures of Priscilla, Queen of the Desert* and became our biggest box-office name with the *Lord of the Rings* and *Matrix* trilogies.

Peter Weir
Sydney-born director Weir won an AFI for *Gallipoli*, BAFTAs for *Dead Poets Society, The Truman Show* and *Master and Commander*, and was Oscar-nominated for *Green Card* and *Witness*, but he is best remembered here for restarting our film industry in 1975 with *Picnic at Hanging Rock.*

Jana Wendt
Melbourne-born presenter and interviewer, Wendt's intense manner and dramatic cheekbones made her a TV drawcard

since the early 1980s for *60 Minutes*, *A Current Affair*, and ABC and SBS news programs. In 2006 Channel 9 paid her $2 million to go quietly from her hosting job on *Sunday*.

David Wenham
Sydney-born actor Wenham won an AFI for *Gettin' Square* and a Logie for *SeaChange*, and hit world eyes in the *Lord of the Rings* and *Van Helsing*.

Sam Worthington
Perth-born, NIDA-trained player of strong silent types, he launched his Hollywood career in 2009 with the big budget fantasies *Terminator Salvation*, *Avatar* and *Clash of the Titans*.

Geoffrey Gurrumul Yunupingu
Northern Territory-born singer-songwriter, Yunupingu has been blind since birth. He sings in the languages of the Yolngu people of Arnhem Land, and in 2008 won the ARIA award for Best World Music Album.

POLITICIANS

Tony Abbott
London-born former trainee for the priesthood and journalist,
Abbott was briefly Minister for Health in the Howard
government, when he appeared to moderate his strongly
anti-abortion views. In 2009 he published a manifesto called
Battlelines, apparently designed to position himself as a future
leader of the Liberal Party.

Joh Bjelke-Petersen
Premier of Queensland from 1968 to 1987, Bjelke-Petersen's
National–Country Party held power due to a gerrymander:
the size of electorates meant country members needed fewer
voters than city members to win a seat. He presided over
police corruption and intensive development, favouring
roads through rainforests and oil drilling on the Great
Barrier Reef.

Brian Burke
Labor Premier of Western Australia from 1983 to 1988, he
involved his government in a series of business deals which
earned the nickname 'WA Inc'. After a Royal Commission
investigated him, he spent seven months in gaol in 1994
for rorting his travel expenses while in office. He became
a lobbyist who arranged deals between entrepreneurs and
politicians, both Labor and Liberal, but in the mid-2000s, the
WA government banned ministers from associating with him.

Peter Costello
Liberal treasurer between 1996 and 2007, Costello is
considered by some conservatives to be the greatest prime

minister Australia never had. He waited patiently for John Howard to retire so he could assume the Liberal leadership, but became an Opposition backbencher when Howard lost the 2007 election. In 2009 Costello announced he would retire at the next election, thereby relieving Malcolm Turnbull of his strongest rival for leadership. But he'll be back.

Don Dunstan
Labor premier of South Australia from 1970 to 1979, Dunstan continued South Australia's tradition of social reform when he legalised abortion and homosexuality, and introduced consumer protection laws. He once wore pink shorts in parliament.

Malcolm Fraser
Liberal prime minister from 1975 to 1983, Fraser is best known for pro-environment views and for appearing without pants in the lobby of a hotel in Memphis, Tennessee, one morning in 1986, after apparently being drugged and robbed. Those who were enraged by his causing the dismissal of Gough Whitlam in 1975 have since forgiven him because of his humanitarian work on behalf of refugees.

Julia Gillard
Considered the person most likely to be the first female prime minister of Australia, Gillard, the leftie lawyer with the grating accent and flaming red hair, changed during 2009 into Julia the elegant honey blonde who had no trouble running two huge federal departments—Education and Industrial Relations—while slicing up the Liberal Party in parliament.

Bob Hawke
Labor prime minister from 1983 to 1991, Hawke was more famous for charisma, crying on television, beer drinking and womanising than for political decisions.

Joe Hockey
Best known for appearing as a jovial debater against Kevin Rudd on the TV program *Sunrise* before the 2007 elections, Hockey was briefly Minister for Employment and Workplace Relations in the Howard government and became Shadow Treasurer when Malcolm Turnbull became Opposition Leader in 2008. In late 2009, he began a series of speeches entitled 'In Defence of God', apparently trying to prove he's more than a big boofy bloke and has The Vision to lead his party.

John Howard
Howard became Liberal prime minister in 1996, and is best known for introducing a 10 per cent Goods and Services Tax, committing Australian troops to join America in Iraq, getting tough on unions and would-be immigrants and expressing his political ambition as to make Australians 'relaxed and comfortable'. He lost government and his seat in 2007.

Paul Keating
Labor treasurer from 1983 and prime minister from 1991 to 1996, Keating introduced land rights for Aboriginal people and economic reforms that allowed business and banks to flourish, but alienated voters with his apparent arrogance.

Robert Menzies
Founder of the Liberal Party and prime minister from 1949 to 1965, Menzies was a father figure in a serious suit and a symbol of stability for a nation undergoing social change.

Henry Parkes

Premier of New South Wales in the 1870s and 1880s, Parkes was a campaigner for free public education and the federation of the colonies into a single nation, but did not live to see his plan fulfilled.

Graham Richardson

As secretary of the NSW Labor Party in the 1970s, he became legendary as 'the numbers man' who would do 'whatever it takes' (the title of his autobiography) to achieve party goals. He became a Senator in the 1980s and served as Minister for the Environment, then Social Security, then Health, before resigning to become a political commentator and lobbyist. He continues to be a powerbroker for the Labor Party and for businessmen and developers.

Kevin Rudd

A former diplomat (who speaks Mandarin), Rudd became prime minister in 2007 and immediately issued an apology to Aboriginal people and signed the Kyoto protocol on climate change. Since coming to power, he has been working to move his image from nerd to ocker by the use of archaic Australianisms such as 'Fair shake of the sauce bottle, mate', 'We've all had to drive the porcelain bus at some stage' and 'You'd have to be blind freddy not to see . . .'

Malcolm Turnbull

The aggressive former leader of the Republican movement, Turnbull became leader of the Liberal Party in 2008. Only his abrasive personality can keep him from reaching his lifelong goal of becoming prime minister. For years he has been dogged by rumours that in his younger days he strangled a girlfriend's cat, though he convincingly denied this in 2009.

Gough Whitlam

Labor prime minister from 1972 to 1975, Whitlam was elected with a program of radical reform after 23 years of conservative government. He moved too fast and was dismissed by the governor-general, John Kerr, after the opposition, under Malcolm Fraser, blocked the budget.

ARTISTS

John Coburn
An abstract painter born in 1925, Coburn designed the Sun and Moon tapestry curtains of the Sydney Opera House.

Patrick Cook
Australia's most savage political and sociological cartoonist, Cook drew for *The National Times*, *The Australian Financial Review* and *The Bulletin* (until it closed in 2008).

Grace Cossington Smith
Van Gogh-influenced Cossington Smith established the Modern Movement in Sydney. She died in 1984.

Philip Cox
An adventurous architect who specialises in big public structures, Cox is behind such landmarks as the Sydney Football Stadium, Sydney's Darling Harbour Exhibition Centre and Yulara Resort near Uluru.

Denton Corker Marshall (DCM)
An architecture and design firm, DCM has, since 1972, transformed the look of the southern capital via the Melbourne Museum, the Exhibition Centre and a 'gateway' of coloured rods sticking up at an angle over the airport freeway. They also designed Brisbane Square, the Museum of Sydney and the Macquarie and Phillip Towers in Sydney. The partners' first names are John, Bill and Barrie.

Ken Done
Done's colourful designs for million-selling tourist souvenirs have overshadowed his more serious paintings.

Max Dupain
His photos of sunbathers and city life became part of the visual
definition of Australia. He died in 1992.

Walter Burley Griffin
An American disciple of Frank Lloyd Wright, Griffin designed
Canberra, the New South Wales town of Griffith, the
Melbourne suburbs of Heidelberg and Eaglemont, and the
Sydney suburb of Castlecrag. He died in 1937.

Pro Hart
Born and based in Broken Hill, Hart painted the colours and
creatures of the Australian desert and did the occasional TV
commercial for carpet cleaners. He died in 2006.

Rover Thomas Joolama
Joolama began using earth pigment on board in the
Kimberley region of Western Australia. He died in 1996.
His works now fetch up to $1 million.

Emily Kame Kngwarreye
A ceremonial painter of rock and bark from Utopia,
200 kilometres east of Alice Springs, Kngwarreye began using
modern materials to paint desert life after she turned 70. She
died in 1996.

Colin Lanceley
Since the 1960s, Lanceley has blended sculpture and painting
into three-dimensional works.

Bill Leak
He draws vicious political caricatures for *The Australian*
newspaper, and paints serious portraits for the Archibald Prize

competition which, he says, he has lost more times than any living artist.

Michael Leunig

Leunig is a whimsical cartoonist, pop philosopher and creator of eccentric characters. He has produced books, TV animations, and illustrations for *The Age* and the *Sydney Morning Herald* newspapers.

Norman Lindsay

Best known for shocking polite society through painting, etching and sculpting naked ladies at his Blue Mountains home near Sydney, Lindsay lives on as the creator of *The Magic Pudding*. He died in 1969.

Frederick McCubbin and Tom Roberts

They set up an artists' colony outside Melbourne in the 1890s and were the first to capture the real colours of the Australian bush, founding the Heidelberg School of Australian impressionism which has influenced landscape painting to this day. McCubbin died in 1917, Roberts in 1931.

Glenn Murcutt

Murcutt's low-rise architectural projects, using materials such as corrugated iron to give an outback appearance, are designed to blend into the environment. In 1992, he won the Alvar Aalto Medal in Finland and in 2001 the international Pritzker Prize.

Sidney Nolan

He painted in series, showing how a place or a story changed over time, and is best known for his Ned Kelly series. He died in 1992.

John Olsen

A painter of outback landscapes, Olsen won the Sulman Prize in 1989 and the Archibald Prize in 2005 for a self-portrait (in an outback landscape).

Bruce Petty

Petty is the nation's most uncompromising, complex and perceptive political cartoonist, originally for *The Australian* and now for *The Age*.

Harry Seidler

An architect of Austrian background, Seidler pioneered the skyscraper in Sydney with Australia Square Tower, the Blues Point Tower, the Horizon Building and the MLC Centre. He died in 2006.

Jeffrey Smart

Smart's paintings are detailed urban scenes approaching 'hyperrealism'. He lives in Tuscany.

Clifford Possum Tjapaltjarri

Tjapaltjarri's dot paintings, which tell elaborate dreaming stories, started the craze for Aboriginal art. He died in 2002.

Brett Whiteley

Best known for heroin addiction and big blue harbour scenes, Whiteley won the Archibald Prize in 1978. He died in 1992.

Cathy Wilcox

Drawing single-column gags for the *Sydney Morning Herald* and *The Age*, Wilcox is the nation's sharpest political cartoonist on a small scale.

PIONEERS OF A NEW AUSTRALIA

Stephanie Alexander
After running Stephanie's, Melbourne's most interesting restaurant, for 21 years, Alexander retired from daily cooking and set about writing the bible of ingredients available in Australia and techniques learned from the multitude of cultures that have joined our population. *The Cook's Companion*, first published in 1996 and revised in 2004, is 816 pages long and has sold half a million copies.

Geoffrey Atherden
Australia's most thoughtful and original TV comedy writer, Atherden began with scripts for *The Aunty Jack Show* in the early 1970s and went on to win multiple awards for creating the sitcoms *Mother and Son* and *Grass Roots*.

Circus Oz
Replacing animal acts with rock music and slapstick with political satire, Circus Oz started in Melbourne in 1978 and by 2005 had performed in 26 countries, stimulating an international boom in 'physical theatre'. From the founding members only Tim Coldwell still performs with the troupe, but the newer acrobats share the original philosophy.

John Clarke
Although born in New Zealand and still sounding like it, Clarke is Australia's 21st-century court jester, interviewed regularly by Bryan Dawe on *The 7.30 Report* in the guise of the most ridiculous politician of the day. His satirical TV series *The Games* anticipated most of the hypocrisy that happened during the 2000 Olympics.

Cheong Liew

Malaysian-born of Chinese parents, Cheong learned to cook
in Greek and French restaurants in Adelaide and introduced
the East meets West or 'fusion cuisine' craze to Australia in
the 1980s. Still experimenting at The Grange restaurant in
Adelaide, he says:

> To do fusion properly a chef should be fluent in five
> culinary languages. Fusion demonstrates what we have
> achieved as humans in terms of the marriage and harmony
> of ingredients as well as people and cultures—it's really
> about multiculturalism in our society.

Hector Crawford

Using the radio production house he founded in Melbourne in
1946, Crawford became the first independent maker of drama
for Australian television, generating series such as *Consider Your
Verdict, Homicide, The Box, Cop Shop, Division 4, All the Rivers
Run* and *The Sullivans*. He died in 1991. His risky vision for
Australian drama was first vindicated in 1966, when news came
through that *Homicide* was out-rating a popular US series called
The Fugitive, and the TV critic Harry Robinson wrote:

> The importance, of course, is not that *Homicide* is
> doing well, but rather that Australians may at last be
> willing to consider their own people with their own ways
> worth watching. Till now, as any showman will tell you,
> Australians have preferred to watch anybody but their own
> kind, no matter what the quality. Perhaps we have grown
> up enough to give ourselves a fair go.

Serge Dansereau

A French-Canadian chef hired to build an international
reputation for Sydney's Regent Hotel, Dansereau arrived

in 1981 to find a dearth of diversity in our salads. Bored by iceberg lettuce, he experimented with imported seeds and used the hotel's buying power to encourage growers to plant such unfamiliar leaves as rocket, chervil, endive, radicchio, cos and regency (named in his honour). Other restaurants and retailers took up his clean green cause.

Collette Dinnigan

Born in New Zealand, Dinnigan started as a lingerie designer but found her customers were wearing her slips as dresses. She launched her own fashion label in Sydney in 1990, had a ready-to-wear parade in Paris in 1995 and now her finely beaded evening gowns are seen on red carpets around the world.

Gino di Santo

Arriving in 1952 from southern Italy, di Santo noticed a few gaps in our eating opportunities and proceeded to import pasta, sauces, wine, cappuccino machines and gelato makers. His Melbourne-based providore business, Enoteca Sileno, introduced Australians to extra virgin olive oil, balsamic vinegar, rice specially grown for risotto and fresh truffles.

Margaret Fulton

Starting as a demonstrator for the gas company in the 1950s, Fulton found she had a knack for explaining recipes to nervous homemakers. She created accessible but adventurous food sections for *Woman's Day* and *New Idea* and *The Margaret Fulton Cookbook*, published in 1968, sold 1.5 million copies. She gave confidence and inspiration to three generations of Australian cooks.

Akira Isogawa

Visiting Australia from Japan on a working holiday in 1986,
Isogawa thought he might make a few bucks by reworking
kimonos to suit Western bodies, and ended up staying and
creating a new style of Japanese/Australian-global design.

Dare Jennings

A surfer who started a clothing line for teenagers called
Mambo in 1984, Jennings encouraged artists to design shirts
that might offend the occasional grandmother. 'We are really
the only designers who reflect Australian culture in any kind
of hip way,' he said. 'It's colourful, it's provocative, but it's
not harbour bridges and bloody kangaroos. We like to take
the piss out of people.' When he sold the business in 2001, it
had become an international youth culture empire offering
hats, pants, watches, bikes, posters and recordings. Other surf
labels such as Quiksilver, Billabong and Rip Curl are just pale
imitations.

Jenny Kee

Of Chinese, Italian and English background, Kee grew up
at Sydney's Bondi Beach, experienced 'Swinging London' in
the 1960s and in 1974 'started designing jumpers with this
whole idea of having this real Australian flavour . . . hand
knitting beautiful things and then putting these wonderful
Australian images on them'. Then she began painting
Australian animals, fish, flowers and birds and printing them
on silk. Her company, Flamingo Park, found international
fame when Diana Spencer wore her jumpers.

Graham Kennedy

Bursting onto Melbourne television in 1957, Kennedy
smashed the *Tonight Show* mould before it was even set.

Nothing was sacred and all that mattered was getting a laugh, so he mocked his sponsors, his bosses and his audience. Appearing and disappearing in a variety of TV guises until his retirement in 1991, he embodied the larrikin we like to think lies in every Australian. He died in 2005.

Jennice and Raymond Kersh
Opening their restaurant Edna's Table in Sydney in 1981, the brother and sister team of chef Raymond and host Jennice worked to show Australians the pleasure of indigenous ingredients such as kangaroo, crocodile, bush tomatoes, quandongs and warrigal greens. As Jennice put it:

> 'It just seemed natural and normal to include native spices and vegetables and meats among the range of things Australians would eat, but it turned out to be much tougher than we expected. Australians seem to have a cultural cringe about their own ingredients before they've even tasted them. We're not interested in being a tourist gimmick. We think eating your own food is part of your sense of place.'

Gilbert Lau
Appointed as host of Melbourne's Flower Drum restaurant in 1975, Lau surprised Australians with the notion that Chinese food could be much more than suburban takeaway. He showed how ancient dishes could be matched with modern wines, and how Cantonese cooking warranted as much analysis as French haute cuisine. He retired in 2004.

Eddie Mabo
A man of the Mer people of Murray Island in the Torres Strait, Mabo brought a case to the High Court which, in 1992,

created the precedent for Aboriginal land rights. The court overturned the doctrine known as 'terra nullius', which said Australia had been 'empty' before white settlement, and ruled that Aboriginal and Torres Strait Islander peoples could claim ownership of their land if they proved continuous settlement since the 18th century. Mabo died six months before his victory was announced.

Hugh Mackay

A researcher into social attitudes since the 1970s, Mackay has a unique talent for assessing the mind and mood of the nation. Before him, Australians were rarely self-analytical. His newspaper columns and his 1993 book *Reinventing Australia* showed us how we were changing.

Oz editors

In 1963 Richard Walsh, Richard Neville and Martin Sharp launched a satirical magazine called *Oz*. In 1964 they were each sentenced to six months' gaol for obscenity (after publishing language and cartoons deemed offensive). The overturning of their conviction on appeal helped to break down the censorship imposed by Australian authorities on literature and art. Sharp and Neville founded a London edition of *Oz*, while Walsh moved into publishing.

Beppi Polese

Trained as a waiter in the great hotels of Italy, Polese reached Australia in 1952 and was shocked at how little pleasure we took in eating. He opened Beppi's in East Sydney in 1956 and set about converting Australians to weird ingredients such as mussels, calamari, eggplant, capsicum and artichokes. With his restaurant now in its fifty-fifth year, he's still there every lunchtime cajoling customers to 'just give this a try'.

Richard Smart

Trained in agricultural science at Sydney University in the 1960s, Smart became the world's most respected viticulturalist, with consulting rooms in Tasmania, Portugal, Peru and the United States. His book *Sunlight Into Wine* is an industry bible and he is credited with raising the drinking standards of 25 nations.

Working Dog

A loose collection of writers and actors based in Melbourne, Working Dog got together in the 1980s for the ABC TV comedy *The D-Generation* then created the movies *The Castle* and *The Dish*; the TV shows *Frontline*, *A River Somewhere*, *All Aussie Adventures*, *The Panel* and *Thank God You're Here*; and the spoof travel guides *Molvania*, *Phaic Tan* and *San Sombrero*. The members are Tom Gleisner, Santo Cilauro, Michael Hirsh, Jane Kennedy and Rob Sitch.

Mandawuy Yunupingu

A man of the Gumatj clan of north-east Arnhem Land, Yunupingu got a degree in education and became the first Aboriginal person to be appointed as a school principal (at Yirrkala on the Gove Peninsula, Northern Territory), and in 1986 formed the rock band Yothu Yindi. Their song 'Treaty', using didgeridoo, bilma (clapsticks), electric guitars and drums, became a world hit in 1991 and the federal government named Yunupingu Australian of the Year in 1992.

Giuseppe Zuzza

Trained as a waiter in north-east Italy, Zuzza arrived in Australia in 1976 with ambition and a recipe. The recipe, borrowed from his friends at El Toula restaurant in the town of Treviso, involved coffee-soaked sponge, mascarpone, chocolate and Tia Maria liqueur. It was called 'tiramisu' (pick-me-up). Zuzza introduced it at Darcy's restaurant in Paddington, Sydney, and then at his own place, The Mixing Pot, in Glebe, Sydney. As other restaurateurs copied him, tiramisu spread across the country, and some form of it is now in every suburban bistro and supermarket. Its success symbolises the internationalisation of our tastes. If lamingtons represent the old Australia, the new Australia is tiramisu.

WHAT'S NEXT

THE SELF-CONCEPT

Two terms became fashionable in Australia's cultural conversations during the Noughties: **'journey'** and **'village'**. All of us are on the first and living in the second. Or we like to think we are. Of course, we could be kidding ourselves. Australians have a bit of a history of self-delusion.

It was the poet Banjo Paterson who first drew attention to the disconnect between our self-image and the reality of the way we live. In 'Clancy of the Overflow' he wrote of the sweet life of the drover, who enjoys the murmuring breezes, the lowing cattle, the vision splendid of the sunlit plains extended, and at night the wondrous glory of the everlasting stars. When that was published (1889), Australians liked to think of themselves that way—**sunbronzed pioneers of a wide brown land**. In the second half of the poem, Paterson begged to differ. He knew that most Australians, even that long ago, were actually breathing the fetid air and gritty of the dusty, dirty city, and seeing the pallid faces of hurrying people who shoulder one another in their rush and nervous haste.

But Paterson failed to shake his readers out of their delusion. Australians stuck with that idyllic but imaginary self-concept for another 100 years. In 1977, when we held a referendum on what should be our national anthem, we voted for a hymn to the same rural identity, portraying a land abounding in nature's gifts, golden soil, and boundless plains to share—if not actually live on. (Mind you, we didn't have a lot of choice—the alternatives were the tale of a suicidal sheep thief and a prayer to save a monarch 17 000 kilometres away).

In 1981, a new candidate for national song arrived, in the form of a TV commercial which described the national identity as 'Football, meat pies, kangaroos and Holden cars'. Australians couldn't stop singing it, even when they learned that it was a straight lift from an American jingle which listed 'baseball, hot dogs, apple pies and Chevrolet'. The advertising agency had done its research on our mindset.

Politicians and pundits kept playing on the antiquated image, even in the 1980s. They referred to their critics as 'chardonnay socialists' or 'the latte set' or 'Balmain basketweavers', pushing the assumption that people who lived in the city and drank wine or coffee were somehow unpatriotic, because **real Australians** drank beer or tea and lived on farms with big families. In reality, 80 per cent of Australians were living in cities, wine consumption was soaring as beer consumption plummeted, and coffee had replaced tea as the national drink in the 1970s.

The first milestone in our journey of self-discovery didn't become apparent until the 1990s. The sign that Australians were finally embracing an urban identity was our obsession with a TV sitcom called *Friends*. It was a success in America, but it was a far bigger success in Australia, where it was the most watched series for the last three years of the 20th century and the first three years of the 21st century.

Clever scripts and pretty actors are not enough to explain this. My theory is that *Friends* reached deep into the national psyche and showed Australians what they wanted to be at that time: **single urban coffee drinkers** with a strong support network and complicated love lives. That image was a lot closer to reality than the bush family myth — by the 90s Australians *had* started marrying later (or not at all) and divorcing earlier. But it differed from reality in two ways: 1) Most of us were not as young and free as the sexy 20-somethings of *Friends*. In fact, 50 per cent of the population were over the age of 36. 2) Very few of us lived in inner-city apartments like Ross, Rachel, Joey, Chandler, Phoebe and Monica.

Although Australia is often described as the most urbanised nation on earth, it would be more accurate to say we're the most suburbanised nation on earth. Some 85 per cent of Australians live in suburbs within 50 kilometres of the sea, and of that 85 per cent, 90 per cent live in houses with three or more bedrooms. We may be coffee addicts, but Manhattan Island we ain't.

The next stage in our journey was apparent in our viewing habits during 2005. That year, one in fourteen American households were fans of a new series called *Desperate Housewives*. In Australia, one in every seven households were fans. What was *Desperate Housewives* about? Life in the village. In their comfortable four-bedroom homes, the residents of Wisteria Lane didn't concern themselves with issues such as terrorism and global financial movements. They looked inwards. Everything happened within their own small universe—they met for coffee, they mowed their lawns, they drove to the shops on the corner, they had affairs with each other, and occasionally they got murdered. What's that if not a portrait of **the typical Australian suburb**—or what we like to think is the typical Australian suburb.

In August of 2005, the social analyst Hugh Mackay released a report based on discussions with sixteen focus groups of ordinary Australians. He said: 'People seem more edgy, angry and stressed. There is growing concern about the state of Australian society: rougher, tougher, more competitive, less compassionate . . . A high divorce rate, a low birthrate and the phenomenon of the shrinking household are destabilising the traditional position of the nuclear family, but driving people to forge closer connections with friends and neighbours. It is no accident that the word "**village**" is in such vogue in contemporary Australia: the concept of village life is intensely appealing to people who are feeling cut off from their families or at risk of being socially isolated.'

Mackay added that the people in his focus groups 'engaged in such lively discussion of media content and media-related events as to suggest our new "guiding story" may be coming to us via pop culture rather than from the traditional legendary mythologies of politics and religion'.

So naturally we were besotted with *Desperate Housewives*. They were Our Story. They had joined our journey, and we had joined theirs. The only catch was that the Despos were Americans—so we couldn't identify with them 100 per cent. That problem was solved in 2008, with the advent of a show called *Packed to the Rafters*. It's about grown-up children coming back to share village life with their 40-something parents in a street not very different from Wisteria Lane. In 2009 it attracted the same kind of audiences as *Friends* and *Desperate Housewives* in their heydays.

In 2009, the Rafter family shared the ratings honours with *MasterChef*, a talent quest won by an occasionally desperate housewife named Julie Goodwin. The show's finale was the most watched non-sports program of the Noughties. The kindly approach of the judges and the cooperative behaviour of the competitors suggested Australian viewers were in the mood for nurturing generosity. Goodwin became earth mother for the nation.

There was, however, another contender in the late Noughties for the title of Popular Culture Symbol of Australia's Image. That was *Underbelly*, a dramatisation of the drug dealing, corruption and murders committed in Melbourne and Sydney between the 1970s and the 1990s. **A nation founded by criminals** had become fascinated by crime adventures.

Our reaction seemed to include a perverse kind of pride. Look at how Channel 9 worded the media release announcing the third season of *Underbelly* planned for 2010: 'Sydney, Kings Cross, 1989. The cops were bent and the crims were cool. And together they ran the most exciting street in Australia. Strippers, gamblers, gunmen, dealers, bouncers, bagmen — they all came to the Golden Mile . . . *Underbelly: The Golden Mile* is the story of the excesses of the empire, the collapse of the empire, and the ultimate victory of strong and honest police . . . seen through the eyes of some of the most sexy, charming, corrupt and deadly people of the time.'

Is that us in 2010 — cool, sexy, corrupt and deadly models of gangster chic? It doesn't necessarily clash with Banjo Paterson's portrait: 'With their eager eyes and greedy, and their stunted forms and weedy . . . townsfolk have no time to grow, they have no time to waste.'

So as we start our journey into the decade we'll presumably call The Teens, Australians have a choice between two paths — towards city slickness or towards village values. Probably we'll take both.

THE SUM OF US

The average adult in this country has one breast and one testicle, and smokes four cigarettes a day. That is presumably who the politicians mean when they pontificate about what **the average Australian** wants, believes, knows to be true and won't stand for.

This fabulous creature emerges when you add up the number of testicles on this continent, or the number of breasts, or the number of cigarettes smoked in a day, and then divide by the number of people aged over 18 — a perfectly respectable way to reach an average, or mean. And you quickly understand why the Bureau of Statistics is wary about using such terms when it reports its findings, preferring to talk about the **median**: the point where half the population has more of the thing being measured and half has less than the thing being measured.

In the mid-Noughties the bureau set out to explain how rich we are in a report called 'Household Wealth and Wealth Distribution'. It revealed that the average household in Australia has assets (house, car, furniture, investments) of $537 000 and liabilities of $69 000 — a **net worth** of $468 000. Those figures make us look pretty well off, evoking **a national snapshot** of smiling mum, dad, two kids and Holden in front of a neat bungalow with a Hills Hoist in the yard. Even without a white picket fence, it gives a reassuring impression of **a lucky country**.

But the bureau warned against such an enthusiastic interpretation:

> While the mean household net worth of all households in Australia was $468 000, the median (i.e. the mid-point when all households are ranked in ascending order of

net worth) was substantially lower at $295 000. This difference reflects the asymmetric **distribution of wealth** between households, where a relatively small proportion of households had relatively high net worth and a large number of households had relatively lower net worth.

What's happening is that the Packers, the Pratts, the Lowys and the Smorgons, with their mansions, planes, yachts and penthouses, are pulling up the average and making the rest of us look better off than we really are. In fact, half of Australia's households are worth less than $295 000—which does not suggest very comfortable living conditions at all. Only eight per cent have net worth above one million dollars, while 17 per cent of households (containing three million people) have net worth below $50 000.

The same problem came up when the bureau looked at how well Australians are providing for their **retirements**. Divide the number of households with super into the total money in super funds and you get an average figure of $85 000. But 25 per cent of households have no super provision of any kind, and among those who do, half have superannuation assets under $35 000.

To indicate how **national wealth** has grown in recent years, the bureau reported that between 1999 and 2004, prices for basic commodities grew 18 per cent, while our spending on recreation (entertainment, sport, holidays) grew 29 per cent, to a household average of $115 a week. But not all households are indulging themselves so furiously. Those in the bottom fifth of earnings spend only $43 a week on recreation.

So it's **all in the way you tell it**. You could say that 51 per cent of Australians have breasts, 49 per cent have testicles, 50 per cent have massively inadequate superannuation cover, 8 per cent are rich, 17 per cent are poor, 20 per cent don't have much fun, and 21 per cent smoke 20 cigarettes a day.

Now you know why you should approach with caution the information you're about to read. What follows is a portrait of a **representative Australian family**, based on a mixture of medians, means and most frequents. It's probable that more than half the families in Australia are a bit like this . . .

Meet Nicole and Michael Smith. He's 39, she's 37. They got married in 1995 after living together for a year, and they have two kids—Matthew, 11, and Emily, 8. Michael is 175 centimetres tall and weighs 82 kilograms but, if asked, would estimate he weighs 80 kilograms. Nicole is 161 centimetres tall and weighs 67 kilograms, but would say 65.

Michael earns $1200 a week in an administrative job, while Nicole earns $600 working three days a week in a shop. They are paying off a three-bedroom home with a small backyard in a suburb 25 kilometres from the sea. The house cost $500 000, and they still owe $113 000 on their mortgage, which they pay off at $110 a week. But they'll sell up and move to a new house within six years.

They still owe $2700 on their white Holden Commodore and right now they have a total credit card debt of $2000. Between them they lose $6 a week on gambling—a couple of scratchies at the newsagents and the occasional pull on the pokies at the pub when they go for dinner.

All four Smiths were born in Australia, but Nicole's parents were born in Britain. The Smiths wrote 'no religion' on their census form, while Michael's parents wrote Catholic and Nicole's parents wrote Anglican.

Michael's father Ron died of a heart attack last year at the age of 69. Nicole's mother Margaret is recovering from breast cancer. They are starting to think Michael's mother Shirley may need to move to a nursing home.

Before she was married, Nicole had a four-week trip to London. Before he was married, Michael had a two-week trip to Thailand. Each year they drive for three hours up or down the coast and take a five-day beach holiday. The family spent a week in New Zealand last year and is planning a trip to California next year.

The last book Michael read was *The Da Vinci Code*. Nicole buys *Women's Weekly* most months and passes it on to her mother. Each of the Smiths goes to the movies five times a year (together, mostly). Michael goes twice a year to football games. They rent a DVD every two weeks to watch on Saturday or Sunday night. In addition to the DVD player they installed last year, their home contains two TV sets, three mobile phones, a VCR, washing machine, microwave, fridge, dishwasher and computer, which is mainly used by Matthew.

They spend $25 a week on fast food and takeaway— McDonald's, pizza and Thai mostly—and eat out in a restaurant once a month, spending $80. Michael and Nicole spend $25 a week on alcohol, each drinking five glasses of wine (three white, two red) and two cans of beer. They each drink five cups of coffee a week, and two cups of tea.

The Smiths have had two encounters with crime in their lives: once when their car was stolen and once when they came home to discover a break-in, with their VCR and some cash missing.

Nicole takes the Pill. And as to how often they have sex, the information is unreliable. They would tell researchers it's about six times a month.

If you think you now know what the majority of Australians are like, think again. Families with children inhabit only 47 per cent of Australian homes. The nation's other homes contain couples without children, single-parent families, and people living alone (23 per cent and growing).

I described the Smiths because their structure is more common than any other configuration of household. But that claim to fame won't last much longer. The Bureau of Statistics made this revelation in 2004:

Over the next 20 years, couple households without children are projected to become the most common of all family types, overtaking couple families with children in 2016 and comprising 42 per cent of families in 2021.

Australia is changing fast, and *The Little Book of Australia* will be regularly revised to chronicle those changes.

THE LITTLE BOOK OF AUSTRALIA

WHERE TO NOW?

A smart shrink once wrote that to be happy, a human being needs three things: something to do, someone to love and something to look forward to. This book may not be much help with the first two, but here are four suggestions on the next social transformations we can strive for:

The national to-do list

1   Become a republic

2   Amalgamate with New Zealand

3   Fix the coat of arms

4   Abolish the states

Fixing the republic is almost too easy. We need only change the title of our head of state from governor-general to administrator. We've become constipated by the word 'president', which sounds scary because it seems to set up an alternative power base to the prime minister. An administrator, chosen by the government (as now) but no longer in need of rubber stamping from a monarch in another country, would merely open official functions and be available to act as referee if there's an insoluble dispute.

Once we officially control our own destiny, we'll be able to make the **New Zealanders** an offer they can't refuse. The former NZ prime minister Robert Muldoon observed that every time a Kiwi is silly enough to move to Australia, that raises the average IQ of both countries. Yes, they do feel superior to us, and not just because they make Australia's favourite wine (Oyster Bay sauvignon blanc). Their kids perform better than ours in those maths and science tests we discussed on page 18. Their politicians tend to be more interesting than ours.

So we must make this transformation worth their while. We can offer to write into the new Constitution our belief that the smartest person in Australia is John Clarke and the greatest actor is Sam Neill. And we'll need to give them the right to impose their pronunciation on the teaching of English in schools (test phrase: 'Lits git some fush en chups for the cet un the het').

When that's done, we can move to update the brand image we present to the world. Look at this nation's **coat of arms**: a tired old emu and a motheaten kangaroo framing a shield engraved with archaic state insignia. My proposal will update it at minimal cost, while retaining the principles on which it was designed in the first place.

Essentially what you see when you look at the coat of arms is a meal. Both animals on it are edible—the emu best served as prosciutto, the kangaroo best served barbecued, charred on the outside and rare in the middle, with beetroot sauce. The shield functions as a plate. So any proposed addition should be consistent with that culinary theme.

The current CoA notably fails in portraying the close relationship of Australians with the ocean. Our home is girt by sea and 85 per cent of us live within 50 kilometres of it. Immigrants came across the sea, our boundless plains to share, but that, too, is ignored by the CoA. My addition will solve both deficiencies in one blow.

Let's put a third native animal into the scene: an octopus, sitting on top of the shield (where there is currently a star) with some of its arms embracing the kangaroo and some of its arms embracing the emu (which we might need to change to a kiwi to please the New Zealanders).

If you visit the central fish market in any Australian capital city, you will see a peculiar sight: a whole lot of octopus being tossed around in modified cement mixers. Traditionally Mediterranean fisherfolk used to tenderise their octopus by throwing them against rocks, but such is the demand for the leggy beast in trendy eateries that the fishmarkets have had to automate the process.

How Australia has changed. Nobody ate octopus in this country 50 years ago. Fishermen threw them back or used them as bait. Then some Mediterraneans settled in and showed Australians new ways to enjoy themselves. And by the 90s, ponytailed chefs in suburban bistros had made char-grilled chilli-coated octopus a candidate for the title of Australia's national dish.

Immigration transformed this land from one of the dullest places on earth to one of the most interesting places on earth, and that's what our coat of arms should celebrate.

When that's done, we can move to a less symbolic and more practical advance — **simplifying the political structure**. It hangs on one question: Do the state leaders have the courage to put themselves out of a job?

Australia must be the most over-governed nation on the planet. We elect 226 politicians to Canberra (76 senators, 150 members of the House of Representatives). We elect 585 politicians to upper and lower houses in our state and territory parliaments. And we elect 6300 alderfolk to 677 local councils.

That's a total of 7120 elected officials, or one politician for every 3000 people. Along with them come thousands of public servants, all busily contradicting, confusing and duplicating the work of their counterparts in the other tiers of government. As Australia's most interesting prime minister,

Gough Whitlam, observed: 'There are few functions which the state parliaments now perform which would not be better performed by the Australian parliament or by regional councils. The states are too large to deal with local matters and too small and weak to deal with national issues.'

Like our monarchy, the states are a hangover from an age when this continent contained colonies with boundaries drawn up by English bureaucrats who didn't understand the geography. Let's eliminate them, and at the same time amalgamate the 677 councils into 100 regional governments, each representing about 200 000 citizens.

The central government would deal with defence, law enforcement, health, education, and environmental and economic management. The regional bodies, with 20 elected officials each, would be responsible for garbage collection, road maintenance, building regulations, licensing of pubs and casinos, fire protection and community activities.

You can already envisage one useful side-effect of **abolishing the states** and amalgamating the councils—the liberation of a great deal of magnificent real estate (houses of parliament, ministerial offices, treasury buildings, town halls). But let's not be greedy. Instead of selling them off, we should preserve them (as theatres, hospitals, museums, prisons, libraries and colleges).

Then our grandchildren will see that the visionaries of 2012 knew how to respect the past as well as when to move into the future. That's something to look forward to.

HOW UN-AUSTRALIAN ARE YOU?

In 2006 the federal government under John Howard (Liberal Party) introduced what came to be called 'The Values Test' for all immigrants seeking Australian citizenship. It was widely criticised as outdated and irrelevant, because it included questions about historical figures such as the cricketer Don Bradman and the billiards player Walter Lindrum. In 2009 the federal government under Kevin Rudd (Labor Party) published a revised edition of the booklet on which the values test would be based, and limited the questions mainly to details about the Australian legal and political system. Sample questions included: What are the colours of the Australian Aboriginal flag; What is the name given to the party or coalition of parties that wins the second largest number of votes in an election; and What is the name of the legal document that sets out the rules for the government of Australia?(answers on page 248).

This is clearly an improvement on the 2006 test, but for any reader of *The Little Book of Australia*, it is seriously unchallenging. You are now in a position to undertake a quiz on how well you really know the people with whom you share this continent. If you get less than 15 correct, go back and read the book again . . .

The Questions

1   Complete these phrases: 'Face like a . . .'; 'Fair shake of the . . .'; 'As welcome as a . . .'; 'I'll be off like a . . .'; 'Dry as a . . .' (pages 38–39)

2   What is Australia's proportion of Muslims; Catholics; Aboriginal people; people classified as obese or over-weight; people living within 50 kilometres of the sea? (pages 2–3)

3 What three movies and three TV series were seen by the most Australians in the past 50 years? (pages 127, 132, 133)

4 Who is Australia's most liked person; richest man; richest woman? (pages 54–56)

5 Of what do Australians eat 380 million a year? (page 170)

6 What's an Australian man's idea of foreplay? (page 30)

7 What proportion of births is to unmarried mothers? (page 7)

8 What is the national flower; dish; drink; greeting; metaphor? (pages 26–27)

9 What happens every one minute and 12 seconds? (page 6)

10 Rank the five major sports in order of attendance and viewing. (page 126)

11 Rank the four main causes of death in order of frequency. (page 10)

12 What proportion of adults say they feel 'terrible', 'unhappy' or 'mostly dissatisfied' with their lives? (page 12)

13 What's the difference between the cultural cringe and the cultural strut? (page 28)

14 What is Australia's favourite wine; newspaper; cigarette; deodorant; toilet paper? (pages 26, 150, 166)

15 Who invented the Chiko Roll; Vegemite; Grange Hermitage; the Paddle Pop? (pages 65, 69, 74, 173)

16 What happened to Azaria Chamberlain; Harold Holt; Schappelle Corby? (pages 76–77)

17 What do we remember on April 25; June 13; the first Tuesday in November; November 11? (pages 81–82)

18 What do we share with those who've come from across the seas? (page 162)

19 In what years did the first mobile phone/ DVD/ iPod go on sale? (pages 96–97)

20 What do Peter Doherty, Barry Marshall and Howard Florey have in common? (page 191)

The Answers

Answers to the government's questions: Black, red and yellow; The Opposition; The Australian Constitution.

1 '. . . dropped pie'; '. . . sauce bottle'; '. . . fart in a two man sub'; 'a bucket of prawns in the sun'; '. . . dead dingo's donga'.

2 1.7% of the population; 26%; 2.5%; 54%; 85%.

3 *The Sound of Music*; *Crocodile Dundee*; *Star Wars*; *Roots*; *Holocaust*; *Homicide*.

4 Hugh Jackman; Anthony Pratt; Gina Rinehart.

5 Tim Tams.

6 Are you awake, love?

7 32%.

8 The golden wattle, spaghetti bolognese, cappuccino, G'day, The Magic Pudding.

9 There is a net gain of one more Australian resident (through births and immigration)

10   AFL, rugby league, tennis, cricket, horse racing.

11   Heart disease, cancer, strokes, lung diseases.

12   3.5%.

13   The belief, now declining, that Australia can never do anything as well as the British or the Americans; the belief, now growing, that we have nothing to learn from the rest of the world.

14   Oyster Bay sauvignon blanc; *The Sunday Telegraph*; Winfield; Rexona; Kleenex cottonelle.

15   Frank McEnroe; Cyril Callister; Max Schubert; Edwin Street.

16   Taken by a dingo at Ayer's rock; lost swimming off a beach near Melbourne; arrested arriving in Bali with marijuana in her boogie board bag.

17   Anzac Day (landing of Australian troops in Turkey in 1915); an English monarch's birthday; the Melbourne Cup horse race; Armistice Day in 1918 and the dismissal of PM Gough Whitlam by the governor-general in 1975.

18   Boundless plains.

19   1986, 1997, 2002.

20   The Nobel Prize.

INDEX

Melbourne 13, 68, 86, 87, 91
Melbourne Cup 68, 81, 87, 175, 177
Meldrum, Ian 'Molly' 177, 207
men 10, 17
Men At Work 95, 144, 174
mental disorders 3, 11
Menzies, Robert 90, 93, 106, 108, 215
Metcalf, Donald 193
metric system 94
Micallef, Shaun 207
microsurgery 49
Middle East 2
Midnight Oil 142, 143, 146, 174, 181
milk bar 90
Miller, George 207
Milton, Michael 189
Minogue, Kylie 33, 139, 178, 208
Mitchell, Radha 75
mobile phones 3, 96
Mole, Kylie 41, 178
Mombassa, Reg 67
Monash, John 105
Morant, Breaker 160
Mortein 67, 91, 167
Mother and Son 135, 222
Moulin Rouge 130, 206
movies 88, 118, 124, 127–31
Mulesing 49
Mundey, Jack 183
Murcutt, Glen 220
murder 16
Murdoch, Lachlan 78
Murdoch, Rupert 92, 95, 195, 197, 198
Muriel's Wedding 71, 96, 130, 202, 203, 204

Murray, Les 197
music 138–47
Muslims 2
My Country 156
'My Island Home' 147
mysteries 76

N
Namitjira, Albert 92
national parks 87, 95
National Party 91, 183
native title 96
Neighbours 74, 95, 146, 178, 203
Neill, Sam 208, 243
netball 126, 189
New Guinea 16
New Holland 84
New South Wales 84
New Zealand 242
newspapers 85, 86, 125, 150
Newton, Bert 208
Newton-John, Olivia 142
Nitschke, Philip 183
Nobel Prize winners 94, 191, 192
Nolan, Sidney 220
Norman, Greg 189
North Korea 91
Northern Territory 89
Nossal, Gus 193
Noyce, Phillip 209
Number 96 134, 174
Nunan, David 197
Nutella 27, 72

O
obesity 3, 11
O'Connor, Frances 209
O'Keefe, Johnny 91, 177
Offset Alpine fire 78